2300 STEPS TO WORD POWER

"All words are pegs to hang ideas on."

— *Henry Ward Beecher*

2300 STEPS TO WORD POWER

PROGRAMMED LEARNING
WITHOUT A MACHINE

AN ARC BOOK

ARCO PUBLISHING COMPANY, INC.
219 Park Avenue South, New York, N.Y. 10003

Tenth Printing, 1978

Published by Arco Publishing Company, Inc.
219 Park Avenue South, New York, N.Y. 10003.

Library of Congress Catalog Card Number: 62-20285
ISBN 0-668-01032-0

Printed in the United States of America

CONTENTS

PROGRAMMED SECTION

SUPPLEMENTARY AIDS TO WORD POWER

PREFACE

VOCABULARY AND SUCCESS

NOT LONG AGO, a very interesting experiment was conducted in the field of vocabulary. The purpose of the study was to determine the relationship, if any, between a person's vocabulary and future success in his profession or occupation. The experimenter was Dr. Johnson O'Connor, Director of the Human Engineering Laboratory of Stevens Institute of Technology.

This was Dr. O'Connor's conclusion from a great number of samplings: **"A large vocabulary is more important than any other measurable factor in the prognosis of success in business or professional endeavor."**

Many research studies show that practically **any intelligent individual can acquire a wide vocabulary, provided he has the will to do so.**

We cannot, at this point, do better than to quote Cassius in Shakespeare's "Julius Caesar": "The fault, dear Brutus, is not in our stars, but in ourselves, that we are underlings."

ABOUT THIS BOOK

THIS BOOK works like a teaching machine, without, however, employing the clumsy and expensive gadgetry often associated with these machines. You have here a book, a programmed book, that is easy to use and effective in its teaching method.

HOW TO USE THIS BOOK

First work with the *odd* pages only—page 1, 3, 5 . . . 219. Let us illustrate the method by turning to page 5. You will notice that there are 10 horizontal "frames" per page, alternately gray and white. The page is also divided, vertically, into a small column at the left and a large column at the right. The column at the left is the correct ANSWER column. We are now concerned with the right-hand column—the QUESTION column—Frame 3, the top frame:

CORRECT   NEW
ANSWER   QUESTION
(previous question)

2. D	3. **ABATE** (A) fish; (B) catch; (C) diminish; (D) embarrass; (E) wound

write *YOUR* answer HERE

In the box—FRAME 3—you will see the synonym question, as above. Note the word you are to define: "ABATE." There are five answer choices: A, B, C, D, and E. In the space provided, write *YOUR* answer.

Now turn to the next odd page—page 7.

Still looking at the top frame, you will see that the CORRECT ANSWER to Frame 3 appears in the small left-hand column.

CORRECT	NEW
ANSWER	QUESTION
(previous question)	

| 3. C | 4. ABET (A) gamble; (B) aid; (C) bite; (D) compromise |

The CORRECT answer to the Frame 3 question is C. Turn back to Frame 3 on page 5 and look at YOUR answer. If you did not answer the question correctly, study the question again until you understand it. Then cross out your incorrect answer and write the correct one. Now go on to Frame 4, page 7.

It is obvious, then, that you will always find the CORRECT ANSWER to a question by turning a page.

Go on in this manner, answering all the consecutively numbered questions in the top row, until you reach the last *odd* page, page 219. Then, return to page 1, this time answering all the questions in the *second* row. When you reach page 219, return again to page 1, and work on the *third* row of frames . . . and so on, until all questions on the right-hand (odd-numbered) pages have been answered.

Now start with page 2, a left-hand (even-numbered) page, and continue to answer all the questions on the left-hand pages – just as you did with the right-hand pages, above.

HOW THIS BOOK IS DIVIDED

The major part of this book consists of 2,190 vocabulary questions of the multiple-choice variety. You will note that the book starts with synonym questions which are divided into three levels: Average Words, Difficult Words, Very Difficult Words. Naturally, you are to start with the questions of the first level—Frame 1, Average Words—and proceed accordingly.

Within each level of synonym questions, the key words are given alphabetically. This has a great advantage if you are using a dictionary (which we strongly urge) with this book. You will find that the alphabetical arrangement is quite a time-saver as you refer to the pages of the dictionary sequentially.

The frames continue with approximately 500 additional vocabulary-building questions in other forms—Analogies, Opposites, and Completions. These vocabulary question types have been included because they appear frequently on the following examinations: Civil Service Tests, College Boards, Scholarship Tests, Graduate Record Examination, Miller Analogy Test, etc.

The Supplement of the book includes "Seven Simple Steps to a Superior Vocabulary," "Word-Building through Latin and Greek," and "Words Often Heard But Not Often Understood."

2300 STEPS TO WORD POWER

1. SYNONYMS
Average Difficulty

Directions: Select the lettered word or phrase nearest in meaning to the capitalized bold-face word.

110. **D**	**111. CONCESSION** (A) nourishment; (B) plea; (C) restoration; (D) similarity; (E) acknowledgment
220. **A**	**221. FRITTER** (A) manipulate; (B) agitate; (C) terrorize; (D) waste
330. **C**	**331. OSTRACIZE** (A) flatter; (B) scold; (C) show off; (D) banish; (E) vibrate
440. **A**	**441. STRINGENT** (A) rigid; (B) threaded; (C) musty; (D) obtainable; (E) avoided
550. **D**	**551. APIARY** (A) cage for primates; (B) collection of beehives; (C) bird cage; (D) eagle's nest
660. **C**	**661. CAVEAT** (A) codicil; (B) unfortunate purchase; (C) warning; (D) agreement in principle
770. **C**	**771. EFFLUENCE** (A) emanation; (B) wealth; (C) vapor; (D) blossom
880. **B**	**881. HECTOR** (A) measure of land; (B) challenger; (C) bully; (D) champion
990. **B**	**991. MAUNDER** (A) weep sentimentally; (B) talk incoherently; (C) flow swiftly; (D) act insincerely

1100. **B**	**1101. PLAIT** (A) handcuff; (B) implore; (C) please; (D) fold
1209. **A**	**1210. SLAKE** (A) sluggish; (B) evade; (C) cinder; (D) quench
1318. **A**	**1319. AMENT** (A) idiot; (B) absentee; (C) moment; (D) plan
1427. **C**	**1428. EPIDEICTIC** (A) oratorical; (B) concise; (C) edifying; (D) comparable
1536. **A**	**1537. MIMESIS** (A) parody; (B) imitation; (C) cacophony; (D) fate
1645. **A**	**1646. SEAR** (A) cut; (B) striped; (C) dried; (D) aged
1754. **B**	**1755. JABBER is to GIBBERISH as QUIDNUNC is to** (A) quisling; (B) gossip; (C) theorist; (D) testator; (E) uncle
1863. **A**	**1864. CATALYST is to CHANGE as ACCELERATOR** **is to** (A) cylinder; (B) inertia; (C) motion; (D) exhaust
1972. **D**	**1973. CRIMINAL : RECIDIVIST : :** (A) crime : prison; (B) dilettante : professional; (C) connoisseur : amateur; (D) probation : parole; (E) divorce : alimony
2081. **A**	**2082. ANTINOMY** (A) name-calling; (B) agreement of two laws; (C) contrary viewpoint; (D) metallic alloy

2. ABASH
(A) strike; (B) deduct; (C) forsake;
(D) confound; (E) enlighten

111.
E

112. CONDONE
(A) sacrifice; (B) contribute generously;
(C) pardon; (D) repent; (E) plot

221.
D

222. FRIVOLITY
(A) lightness; (B) irritability; (C) falseness;
(D) ornamentation; (E) impurity

331.
D

332. OVATION
(A) eggshell; (B) circumference; (C) opening;
(D) slyness; (E) homage

441.
A

442. STUPEFY
(A) subjugate; (B) stun; (C) resect; (D) imprecate

551.
B

552. APLOMB
(A) self-assurance; (B) stodginess; (C) foppishness;
(D) sturdiness

661.
C

662. CAVEAT EMPTOR
(A) beware of the dog; (B) do not enter here;
(C) silence in court; (D) let the buyer beware

771.
A

772. EFFULGENT
(A) radiant; (B) dissembling; (C) animated;
(D) abundant

881.
C

882. HEDONISTIC
(A) classical; (B) ascetic; (C) heinous;
(D) pleasure-loving

991.
B

992. MAVERICK
(A) heavy cudgel; (B) orator; (C) opponent;
(D) unbranded animal

1101. **D**	**1102. PLANGENT** (A) reverberating; (B) pertaining to marine organisms; (C) clamoring; (D) pertaining to the coast
1210. **D**	**1211. SLOE-EYED** (A) of gentle look; (B) almond-eyed; (C) heavy-eyed; (D) black-eyed
1319. **A**	**1320. AMERCE** (A) transact; (B) mulct; (C) despise; (D) fabricate
1428. **A**	**1429. EPIGEAL** (A) living near the ground; (B) repulsive; (C) pertaining to the epiglottis; (D) galvanic
1537. **B**	**1538. MISE EN SCENE** (A) fracas; (B) milieu; (C) view; (D) picture
1646. **C**	**1647. SEBACEOUS** (A) subcutaneous; (B) salacious; (C) fatty; (D) sweaty
1755. **B**	**1756. KEYNOTE is to TONIC as DIAPASON is to** (A) gamut; (B) clef; (C) chord; (D) organ; (E) diaphragm
1864. **C**	**1865. CATAMARAN is to RAFT as TERMAGANT is to** (A) grisette; (B) benedict; (C) spinster; (D) shrew
1973. **B**	**1974. DISCRIMINATE : SEGREGATE : :** (A) select : separate; (B) good : best; (C) sift : unravel; (D) blend : fuse; (E) convict : punish
2082. **B**	**2083. ASYNDETON** (A) periodic in structure; (B) lacking parallelism; (C) faulty in conclusion; (D) inclusion of conjunctions

TURN TO PAGE 7
TOP FRAME (FRAME 4)

2. **D**	**3. ABATE** (A) fish; (B) catch; (C) diminish; (D) embarrass; (E) wound
112. **C**	**113. CONFIRMATION** (A) trust; (B) suspense; (C) encounter; (D) restraint; (E) proof
222. **A**	**223. FULCRUM** (A) spigot; (B) granule; (C) satiated; (D) pivot
332. **E**	**333. PARITY** (A) doubt; (B) equality; (C) fitness; (D) littleness
442. **B**	**443. SUAVE** (A) careful; (B) attractive; (C) foreign; (D) unnatural; (E) polished
552. **A**	**553. APOCRYPHAL** (A) awesome; (B) disease-bearing; (C) of doubtful authority; (D) threatening
662. **D**	**663. CAVIL** (A) fawn; (B) petition; (C) plot; (D) quibble
772. **A**	**773. EGREGIOUS** (A) flagrant; (B) friendly; (C) unintentioned; (D) vicious
882. **D**	**883. HEGEMONY** (A) leadership; (B) rank; (C) conquest; (D) symposium
992. **D**	**993. MAYHEM** (A) maiming; (B) murder; (C) fate; (D) irresolution

TURN TO PAGE 8
TOP FRAME

1102. A	**1103. PLATITUDE** (A) thanksgiving; (B) perception; (C) commonplace; (D) subterfuge
1211. D	**1212. SOBRIQUET** (A) musical comedy actress; (B) nickname; (C) puppet; (D) habitual temperance
1320. B	**1321. AMICE** (A) submit; (B) punish by arbitrary fine; (C) alter by due formal procedure; (D) hooded cape
1429. A	**1430. EPIGRAPH** (A) postscript; (B) tombstone figurine; (C) inscription; (D) duplicating device
1538. B	**1539. MISPRISION** (A) unlawful act; (B) unjust incarceration; (C) evil destiny; (D) supplication
1647. C	**1648. SEMASIOLOGY** (A) logistics; (B) semantics; (C) sociology; (D) petrology
1756. A	**1757. POLTROON is to TERROR as PARANOIAC is to** (A) courage; (B) shyness; (C) persecution; (D) paralysis; (E) responsibility
1865. D	**1866. CINCTURE is to WAIST as SPHINCTER is to** (A) didoes; (B) bone splint; (C) blood clot; (D) orifice
1974. A	**1975. EMULATE : MIMIC : :** (A) slander : defame; (B) praise : flatter; (C) obituary : eulogy; (D) complain : condemn; (E) express : imply
2083. D	**2084. AUSCULTATION** (A) religious veneration; (B) refusal to listen; (C) political intrigue; (D) indoor horticulture

Page 6

3. C	4. ABET (A) gamble; (B) aid; (C) bite; (D) compromise
113. E	114. CONSPECTUS (A) striking; (B) survey; (C) agreement; (D) associate
223. D	224. FUTILITY (A) loyalty; (B) evil; (C) faith; (D) hatred; (E) uselessness
333. B	334. PARLEY (A) discussion; (B) thoroughfare; (C) salon; (D) surrender; (E) division
443. E	444. SUBSIDIZE (A) store for later use; (B) aid with public money; (C) place under military control; (D) check; (E) ridicule in public
553. C	554. APOGEE (A) introductory remarks; (B) nadir; (C) figure of speech; (D) climax
663. D	664. CELIBATE (A) unmarried; (B) leafy; (C) heavenly; (D) servile
773. A	774. ELIDE (A) uncover; (B) loosen; (C) suppress; (D) illuminate
883. A	884. HEGIRA (A) supreme command; (B) small wild animal; (C) system of philosophy; (D) flight
993. A	994. MEAD (A) upland; (B) fermented drink; (C) reward; (D) fallow soil

1103. C	**1104. PLEONASTIC** (A) redundant; (B) erratic; (C) abundant; (D) persuasive
1212. B	**1213. SOLICITUDE** (A) care; (B) salesmanship; (C) sun-worship; (D) desire
1321. D	**1322. ANA** (A) recipes; (B) information; (C) parables; (D) nurses
1430. C	**1431. EPISTAXIS** (A) hierarchy; (B) witticism; (C) nosebleed; (D) classification
1539. A	**1540. MONODY** (A) single vowel; (B) dirge; (C) treatise; (D) self-esteem; (E) warning
1648. B	**1649. SERAGLIO** (A) serape; (B) camel; (C) harem; (D) sultan; (E) sarong
1757. C	**1758. LATITUDE is to LONGITUDE as WARP is to** (A) weave; (B) woof; (C) thread; (D) line; (E) straight
1866. D	**1867. DEBIT is to CREDIT as DENOUEMENT is to** (A) climax; (B) outcome; (C) complication; (D) untying
1975. B	**1976. RESIST : COOPERATE : :** (A) incompatible : oppose; (B) reluctant : averse; (C) command : request; (D) declare : deny; (E) help : aid
2084. B	**2085. BASILIC** (A) fundamental; (B) deadly; (C) slaggy; (D) lowly

4. **B**	**5. ABDICATE** (A) achieve; (B) protest; (C) renounce; (D) demand; (E) steal
114. **B**	**115. CONTEMPLATE** (A) recall; (B) consider; (C) respect; (D) commit; (E) distribute
224. **E**	**225. GARRULOUS** (A) dissipated; (B) interwoven; (C) military; (D) talkative; (E) variegated
334. **A**	**335. PENURIOUS** (A) generous; (B) stingy; (C) poisonous; (D) suffering
444. **B**	**445. SUCCINCT** (A) superfluous; (B) concise; (C) fearful; (D) despicable
554. **D**	**555. APOLOGUE** (A) fable; (B) conclusion; (C) preamble; (D) excuse
664. **A**	**665. CHALICE** (A) necklace; (B) goblet; (C) ecclesiastical garment; (D) mountain hut
774. **C**	**775. EMASCULATE** (A) make clean; (B) unmask; (C) enervate; (D) atrophy
884. **D**	**885. HEINOUS** (A) atrocious; (B) unbelievable; (C) secretive; (D) dangerous
994. **B**	**995. MEED** (A) exigency; (B) reward; (C) fermented drink; (D) noble thought

1104. A	1105. PLETHORA (A) scourge; (B) trope; (C) superfluity; (D) completeness
1213. A	1214. SOMATIC (A) sleepy; (B) corporeal; (C) seminal; (D) psychogenic
1322. B	1323. ANACREONTIC (A) epic; (B) convivial; (C) lawless; (D) colorless; (E) tragic
1431. C	1432. EQUITATION (A) horsemanship; (B) egalitarianism; (C) euphoria; (D) serenity
1540. B	1541. MONOGRAPH (A) signature; (B) treatise; (C) forgery; (D) pillar
1649. C	1650. SERICEOUS (A) grain-like; (B) silky; (C) in order; (D) antagonistic
1758. B	1759. ELEGANCE is to LUXURY as POVERTY is to (A) penury; (B) misery; (C) poorhouse; (D) hunger; (E) paucity
1867. C	1868. OBSTRUCT is to IMPEDE as IMPENETRABLE is to (A) forbearing; (B) hidden; (C) impervious; (D) merciful
1976. C	1977. OPPOSITES *Directions:* Select from the lettered words the word which is most nearly opposite in meaning to the capitalized, bold-face word.
2085. D	2086. BOWDLERIZED (A) uncensored; (B) chopped fine; (C) swallowed whole; (D) criticized severely

5. C	**6. ABHOR** (A) hate; (B) admire; (C) taste; (D) skip; (E) resign
115. B	**116. CONTEMPTUOUS** (A) thoughtful; (B) soiled; (C) dishonorable; (D) scornful; (E) self-satisfied
225. D	**226. GAUNT** (A) stiff; (B) white; (C) repulsive; (D) harsh-sounding; (E) lean
335. B	**336. PERMEATE** (A) permit; (B) impress; (C) penetrate; (D) imperil
445. B	**446. SUFFICE** (A) endure; (B) annex; (C) be foolish; (D) be adequate; (E) eat up
555. A	**556. APOSTASY** (A) defection; (B) affiliation; (C) devotion; (D) revelation
665. B	**666. CHAMP** (A) paw nervously; (B) ram down; (C) chew noisily; (D) restrain forcefully
775. C	**776. EMBRASURE** (A) recess of a door; (B) affectionate gesture; (C) portable stove; (D) gully
885. A	**886. HIRSUTE** (A) depilous; (B) scatter-brained; (C) hairy; (D) heroic
995. B	**996. MEGATON** (A) one million tons; (B) loud tone; (C) amplifier; (D) one thousand pounds

1105. C	**1106. POETASTER**
	(A) canopy over a bed; (B) literary patron; (C) convivial companion; (D) inferior poet

1214. B	**1215. SOPHISTRY**
	(A) verity; (B) wisdom; (C) heresy; (D) fallacy

1323. B	**1324. ANCHORITE**
	(A) slave; (B) fanatic; (C) sailor; (D) Greek; (E) recluse

1432. A	**1433. ERUBESCENT**
	(A) flourishing; (B) eradicating; (C) fading; (D) blushing

1541. B	**1542. MORAINE**
	(A) glacial deposit; (B) hilly country; (C) small island; (D) swamp

1650. B	**1651. SERRIED**
	(A) dried; (B) crowded; (C) ragged; (D) separated

1759. A	**1760. DISCIPLE is to MENTOR as PROSELYTE is to**
	(A) opinion; (B) expedition; (C) leader; (D) football; (E) follower

1868. C	**1869. FELICITY is to BLISS as CONGENIAL is to**
	(A) clever; (B) compatible; (C) fierce; (D) unfriendly

	1978. ECLECTIC
	(A) brilliant; (B) not choosing; (C) short pastoral poem; (D) conclusive

2086. A	**2087. CABALA**
	(A) medieval tribunal; (B) voodoo symbols; (C) published doctrine; (D) conspiratorial gathering

6. **A**	**7. ABOUND** (A) jump about; (B) be plentiful; (C) shorten; (D) forsake; (E) limit
116. **D**	**117. CONTRITE** (A) contrary; (B) trying; (C) penitent; (D) bright
226. **E**	**227. GENIAL** (A) particular; (B) difficult; (C) imaginary; (D) oversized; (E) cheerful
336. **C**	**337. PERTINENT** (A) related; (B) saucy; (C) quick; (D) impatient; (E) excited
446. **D**	**447. SULK** (A) cry; (B) annoy; (C) lament; (D) be sullen; (E) scorn
556. **A**	**557. APOTHEOSIS** (A) glorification; (B) disciplinary action; (C) iconoclast; (D) evil action
666. **C**	**667. CHARY** (A) scorched; (B) frugal; (C) scarce; (D) burnt
776. **A**	**777. EMOLLIENT** (A) swollen; (B) tearful; (C) superficially emotional; (D) softening
886. **C**	**887. HISTRIONIC** (A) eventful; (B) theatrical; (C) recording; (D) emotional
996. **A**	**997. MELLIFLUOUS** (A) mature; (B) flowing smoothly; (C) abundant; (D) morbid

1106. D	1107. POLEMICAL (A) mathematical; (B) astronomical; (C) disputatious; (D) athletic
1215. D	1216. SPECIOUS (A) classified; (B) moneyed; (C) plausible; (D) striking
1324. E	1325. ANELE (A) anoint; (B) subordinate; (C) parallel; (D) excommunicate; (E) curse
1433. D	1434. ESCARPMENT (A) steep slope; (B) trench; (C) fishery; (D) dashboard
1542. A	1543. NACREOUS (A) at the lowest point; (B) shaped like an oriental tobacco pipe; (C) like mother-of-pearl; (D) numbed by drugs
1651. B	1652. SESQUIPEDALIA (A) long words; (B) lame feet; (C) funeral services; (D) bases
1760. C	1761. ARTIFICE is to FINESSE as INEPT is to (A) inefficient; (B) artistic; (C) tricky; (D) insatiable; (E) clever
1869. B	1870. CAUTIOUS is to CIRCUMSPECT as PRECIPITOUS is to (A) deep; (B) flat; (C) high; (D) steep
1978. B	1979. TRUCULENT (A) peaceful; (B) fawning; (C) automotive; (D) unruly
2087. C	2088. CANOROUS (A) extremely hungry; (B) euphoniously sonorous; (C) cacophonous; (D) hound-like

7. B	**8. ABSCOND** (A) detest; (B) reduce; (C) swallow up; (D) dismiss; (E) flee
117. C	**118. CONTROVERSIAL** (A) faultfinding; (B) pleasant; (C) debatable; (D) ugly; (E) talkative
227. E	**228. GENTEEL** (A) unrefined; (B) unbelieving; (C) well-bred; (D) genial
337. A	**338. PERSONABLE** (A) self-centered; (B) attractive; (C) insulting; (D) intimate; (E) sensitive
447. D	**448. SUPERCILIOUS** (A) foolish; (B) needless; (C) callous; (D) haughty
557. A	**558. APPOSITE** (A) appetizing; (B) appealing; (C) appropriate; (D) opposite
667. B	**668. CHAPBOOK** (A) style book used by publishers and printers; (B) small book of popular literature; (C) missal; (D) compendium of usage
777. D	**778. EMOLUMENT** (A) soothing application; (B) compensation; (C) appeasement; (D) reparation
887. B	**888. HISTOLOGY is a branch of** (A) anatomy; (B) historiography; (C) psychiatry; (D) phonology
997. B	**998. MENDACIOUS** (A) living by alms; (B) given to falsehood; (C) hereditary; (D) menial

1107. C	**1108. POLTROON** (A) coward; (B) colonial landowner; (C) fool; (D) low-grade gambling resort
1216. C	**1217. SPOLIATE** (A) decay; (B) besmirch; (C) wind on a bobbin; (D) plunder
1325. A	**1326. ANILE** (A) herbaceous plant; (B) like an old woman; (C) youngish; (D) vivacious
1434. A	**1435. ESCUTCHEON** (A) shield; (B) family history; (C) morals; (D) achievement; (E) blemish
1543. C	**1544. NARIAL** (A) negative; (B) pertaining to the jaw; (C) pelagic; (D) pertaining to the nostrils
1652. A	**1653. SHALLOP** (A) shoal; (B) onion; (C) shellfish; (D) boat
1761. A	**1762. SPLENETIC is to BENIGNANT as ENIGMATIC is to** (A) turbid; (B) pellucid; (C) festoon; (D) opacity; (E) problematic
1870. D	**1871. INQUISITIVE is to INCURIOUS as MANIFEST is to** (A) latent; (B) many-sided; (C) obvious; (D) manipulated
1979. A	**1980. BIBULOUS** (A) biblical; (B) artistic; (C) bookish; (D) non-absorbent
2088. C	**2089. CAVEAT** (A) deception; (B) roe; (C) invitation; (D) seizure

8. **E**	**9. ABSTRUSE** (A) profound; (B) absurd; (C) enormous; (D) ridiculous
118. **C**	**119. CORPOREAL** (A) military; (B) naval; (C) bodily; (D) legal
228. **C**	**229. GHASTLY** (A) hasty; (B) furious; (C) breathless; (D) deathlike; (E) spiritual
338. **B**	**339. PERVERSE** (A) contrary; (B) stingy; (C) unfortunate; (D) hereditary; (E) easygoing
448. **D**	**449. SUPERFICIAL** (A) shallow; (B) unusually fine; (C) proud; (D) aged; (E) spiritual
558. **C**	**559. APPRISE** (A) defeat; (B) pillage; (C) inform; (D) astonish
668. **B**	**669. CHARIVARI** (A) potpourri; (B) mock serenade; (C) court levee; (D) country dance
778. **B**	**779. EMPYREAL** (A) celestial; (B) experimental; (C) exalted; (D) magisterial
888. **A**	**889. HOBSON'S CHOICE** (A) hazardous venture; (B) unwise appointment to office; (C) no choice; (D) decision dictated by self-interest
998. **B**	**999. MENDACITY** (A) embezzlement; (B) solicitation; (C) prevarication; (D) sordidness

1108. A	1109. PORTENTOUS (A) important; (B) portable; (C) intense; (D) ominous
1217. D	1218. SPORADIC (A) generative; (B) occurring occasionally; (C) sporty; (D) of doubtful authenticity
1326. B	1327. ANNULAR (A) living but one growing season; (B) having the form of a ring; (C) income payable at certain intervals; (D) tending to destroy utterly
1435. A	1436. ESTAMINET (A) cottage; (B) boulevard; (C) café; (D) sidewalk; (E) French song
1544. D	1545. NAVE (A) rascal; (B) hub of wheel; (C) altar in church; (D) umbilicus
1653. D	1654. SHAMAN (A) secondary god; (B) idolator; (C) idol- worshipper; (D) image; (E) medicine man
1762. B	1763. FATHER is to DAUGHTER as UNCLE is to (A) son; (B) daughter; (C) son-in-law; (D) niece; (E) aunt
1871. A	1872. FETISH is to TALISMAN as FEALTY is to (A) allegiance; (B) faithlessness; (C) payment; (D) real estate
1980. D	1981. DISCRETE (A) prudent; (B) judicious; (C) joined; (D) stunted
2089. C	2090. CEREMENT (A) death mask; (B) garment for the living; (C) inscription on tomb; (D) refrain in threnody

9. A	**10. ACCELERATE** (A) surpass; (B) cheer; (C) quicken; (D) impede; (E) transport
119. C	**120. CORROBORATE** (A) deny; (B) elaborate; (C) confirm; (D) gnaw; (E) state
229. D	**230. GIRD** (A) surround; (B) appeal; (C) request; (D) break; (E) glance
339. A	**340. PHALANX** (A) bone; (B) membrane; (C) ghost; (D) corpuscle
449. A	**450. SUPERSEDE** (A) retire; (B) replace; (C) overflow; (D) bless; (E) oversee
559. C	**560. ARBITRARY** (A) fair; (B) capricious; (C) angry; (D) impartial
669. B	**670. CHARLATAN** (A) quack; (B) taskmaster; (C) nationalist; (D) servant
779. A	**780. ENCLAVE** (A) colony; (B) enclosure within foreign territory; (C) protectorate; (D) mandated territory
889. C	**890. HOMILY** (A) unpretentiously; (B) sermon; (C) maize food; (D) domestically
999. C	**1000. MENDICANT** (A) merchant; (B) adjuster; (C) prevaricator; (D) beggar

1109. D	**1110. POSEUR** (A) professional model; (B) unsolved problem; (C) guesser; (D) person affected in manner
1218. B	**1219. SPUME** (A) odor; (B) waste; (C) smoke; (D) froth
1327. B	**1328. ANTINOMY** (A) conceptualism; (B) healing herb; (C) contradiction; (D) indulgence; (E) obligation
1436. C	**1437. ESTIVATE** (A) spend the summer; (B) travel eastward; (C) raise; (D) censure
1545. B	**1546. NEBULOSE** (A) indistinct; (B) hypothetic; (C) naught; (D) vitamin
1654. E	**1655. SHARD** (A) fissile rock; (B) pottery fragment; (C) primitive sculpture; (D) stony beach
1763. D	**1764. PISTOL is to TRIGGER as MOTOR is to** (A) wire; (B) dynamo; (C) amperes; (D) barrel; (E) switch
1872. A	**1873. ISLAND : OCEAN : :** (A) pit : orange; (B) filament : bulb; (C) city : nation; (D) water : oasis; (E) pine : grove
1981. C	**1982. POLTROON** (A) brave man; (B) colonial landowner; (C) fool; (D) gambling resort
2090. B	**2091. CICATRICE** (A) smooth surface; (B) house pest; (C) fabulous serpent; (D) summer insect

10. C	**11. ACCENTUATE** (A) emphasize; (B) abbreviate; (C) acclaim; (D) assess
120. C	**121. COUNTERMAND** (A) reaffirm; (B) reconstruct; (C) copy; (D) rescind
230. A	**231. GNARLED** (A) angry; (B) bitter; (C) twisted; (D) ancient; (E) embroidered
340. A	**341. PHASE** (A) expression; (B) concern; (C) adolescence; (D) aspect; (E) embarrassment
450. B	**451. SUPINE** (A) listless; (B) agile; (C) animate; (D) pleading
560. B	**561. ARCANE** (A) obsolete; (B) secret; (C) exalted; (D) curved
670. A	**671. CHAUVINISM** (A) pacifism; (B) political isolationism; (C) exaggerated patriotism; (D) militarism
780. B	**781. ENCOMIUM** (A) compass; (B) oddity; (C) husbandry; (D) praise
890. B	**891. HONORARIUM** (A) liberality; (B) fulfillment; (C) reward; (D) epitaph
1000. D	**1001. MENDICITY** (A) deceit; (B) haggling; (C) hypocrisy; (D) begging

1110. **D**	**1111. POSTPRANDIAL** (A) after dinner; (B) liqueur; (C) twilight; (D) aperitif
1219. **D**	**1220. SPURIOUS** (A) sharply critical; (B) festering; (C) fictitious; (D) goading
1328. **C**	**1329. ANTIPHONY** (A) fallacy; (B) argument; (C) discord; (D) response
1437. **A**	**1438. ESURIENT** (A) certain; (B) hungry; (C) luxurious; (D) foolish
1546. **A**	**1547. NECROPOLIS** (A) paradise; (B) cemetery; (C) mammoth industrial center; (D) small town
1655. **B**	**1656. SIB** (A) error; (B) blood relation; (C) ingestion; (D) weak cry
1764. **E**	**1765. CUBE is to PYRAMID as SQUARE is to** (A) box; (B) Egypt; (C) pentagon; (D) triangle; (E) cylinder
1873. **D**	**1874. FRUIT : ORCHARD : :** (A) tree : forest; (B) fish : sea; (C) lumber : mill; (D) seed : flower; (E) money : cash
1982. **A**	**1983. LAMBENT** (A) cool and moist; (B) warped; (C) riding roughshod; (D) shining brightly
2091. **A**	**2092. CONGENERIC** (A) artificially reproduced; (B) remotely related; (C) carefree in nature; (D) of a different kind

11. **A**	**12. ACCLAIM** (A) discharge; (B) excel; (C) applaud; (D) divide; (E) speed
121. **D**	**122. COVET** (A) shelter; (B) crave; (C) crouch; (D) bargain; (E) hatch
231. **C**	**232. GRAVITY** (A) displeasure; (B) thankfulness; (C) suffering; (D) roughness; (E) seriousness
341. **D**	**342. PHLEGMATIC** (A) sluggish; (B) active; (C) potent; (D) secretive
451. **A**	**452. SURMOUNT** (A) conquer; (B) release; (C) escape; (D) insert; (E) display
561. **B**	**562. ARCHETYPE** (A) prototype; (B) summit; (C) fiend; (D) ecclesiastic
671. **C**	**672. CHOLERIC** (A) irascible; (B) amorphous; (C) optimistic; (D) fatty
781. **D**	**782. ENDEMIC** (A) peculiar to one locality; (B) able to penetrate the skin; (C) swollen; (D) accented on the final syllable
891. **C**	**892. HOVER** (A) poise in flight; (B) swoop to landing; (C) change position; (D) falter
1001. **D**	**1002. MERETRICIOUS** (A) deserving; (B) fawning; (C) imitative; (D) gaudy

1111. A	1112. POSTULATE (A) hanker; (B) delay; (C) demonstrate; (D) assume
1220. C	1221. SQUIB (A) sarcastic saying; (B) pen point; (C) shellfish; (D) young pigeon
1329. D	1330. ANTISTROPHE (A) substitution; (B) dramatic climax; (C) Greek anthem; (D) inverse relation; (E) panorama
1438. B	1439. ETIOLATION (A) ingestion; (B) hardening; (C) wasting away gradually; (D) blanching
1547. B	1548. NECROPSY (A) ornament; (B) disease; (C) narcotic; (D) autopsy
1656. B	1657. SIDEREAL (A) oblique; (B) interplanetary; (C) chimerical; (D) starry
1765. D	1766. PROFIT is to SELLING as FAME is to (A) buying; (B) cheating; (C) bravery; (D) praying; (E) loving
1874. B	1875. ALTITUDE : MOUNTAIN : : (A) height : weight; (B) depth : ocean; (C) mass : energy; (D) latitude : country; (E) incline : hill
1983. C	1984. EXTRINSIC (A) germ-proof; (B) eccentric; (C) uncultivated; (D) internal
2092. D	2093. CONTUMELIOUS (A) compromising; (B) mildly reproachful; (C) laudatory; (D) genuinely contrite

12. C	13. ACCORD (A) opposition; (B) agreement; (C) praise; (D) exclamation; (E) helpfulness
122. B	123. COVETOUS (A) undisciplined; (B) grasping; (C) timid; (D) insincere; (E) secretive
232. E	233. GUILE (A) blame; (B) market; (C) direction; (D) deceit; (E) throat
342. A	343. PHOBIA (A) temper; (B) disease; (C) puzzle; (D) dream; (E) fear
452. A	453. SUSTENANCE (A) nourishment; (B) overabundance; (C) anxiety; (D) equality; (E) alertness
562. A	563. ARCHIPELAGO (A) colonial possession; (B) group of islands; (C) tropical fish; (D) bird of prey
672. A	673. CHRONOLOGY (A) study of maps; (B) fluorescence; (C) time sequence; (D) perpetual calendar
782. A	783. ENERVATED (A) excited; (B) energetic; (C) weakened; (D) brash
892. A	893. HOYDEN (A) bold girl; (B) Indian dwelling; (C) kitchen garbage pile; (D) clodhopper
1002. D	1003. METICULOUS (A) spotted; (B) impeccable; (C) famous; (D) careful

1112. D	**1113. POTABLE** (A) beverage; (B) cheese; (C) preserved food; (D) stew
1221. A	**1222. STAR CHAMBER** (A) secret tribunal; (B) royal manifesto; (C) illegal seizure; (D) special jury
1330. D	**1331. APHASIA** (A) loss of speech; (B) deafness; (C) loss of memory; (D) tonguetiedness
1439. D	**1440. ETIOLOGY** (A) epitome; (B) inertia; (C) cause; (D) ecology
1548. D	**1549. NEOLOGISMS** (A) prehistoric remains; (B) nerve diseases; (C) new words; (D) cave drawings
1657. D	**1658. SIMILITUDE** (A) alloy; (B) resemblance; (C) benefice; (D) personification; (E) alliteration
1766. C	**1767. BINDING is to BOOK as WELDING is to** (A) box; (B) tank; (C) chair; (D) wire; (E) pencil
1875. B	**1876. SUN : DAY : :** (A) moon : dusk; (B) bulb : house; (C) stars : night; (D) heat : summer; (E) earth : axis
1984. D	**1985. CONSENSUS** (A) poll; (B) disharmony; (C) conference; (D) attitude
2093. C	**2094. CUPIDITY** (A) passing fancy; (B) restraint; (C) foolish attraction; (D) make-believe tenderness

13. B	**14. ACME** (A) academy; (B) summit; (C) nadir; (D) ache
123. B	**124. CRAFTY** (A) sly; (B) irritable; (C) seaworthy; (D) operatic; (E) municipal
233. D	**234. GUISE** (A) trickery; (B) request; (C) innocence; (D) misdeed; (E) appearance
343. E	**344. PLACID** (A) public; (B) watered; (C) quiet; (D) established; (E) colorless
453. A	**454. TACITURN** (A) weak; (B) evil; (C) tender; (D) silent; (E) sensitive
563. B	**564. ARCHIVES** (A) shelves; (B) columns; (C) government workers; (D) public records
673. C	**674. CICATRICE** (A) scar; (B) insect; (C) tourniquet; (D) effigy
783. C	**784. ENTOMOLOGY** (A) study of plant fossils; (B) study of relics of man; (C) study of insects; (D) study of derivatives
893. A	**894. HOROLOGE** (A) timepiece; (B) forecast; (C) genealogy; (D) summary
1003. D	**1004. MINATORY** (A) advising; (B) threatening; (C) turret-like; (D) monstrous

1113. A	1114. PRAGMATIC (A) smoothly rehearsed; (B) practical; (C) absolute; (D) bookish
1222. A	1223. STENTORIAN (A) typed; (B) terse; (C) useless; (D) loud
1331. A	1332. APSE (A) proclivity; (B) recess; (C) gibbon; (D) legume
1440. C	1441. EUTHENICS (A) dancing as an expression of emotion; (B) painless death; (C) race improvement; (D) science of heredity
1549. C	1550. NESCIENCE (A) occult knowledge; (B) ignorance; (C) stupor; (D) birth
1658. B	1659. SIROCCO (A) hot, oppressive wind; (B) equatorial tide; (C) desert calm; (D) residue of mist
1767. B	1768. GYMNASIUM is to HEALTH as LIBRARY is to (A) sick; (B) study; (C) books; (D) knowledge; (E) school
1876. C	1877. FOREST : FLORA : : (A) zoo : animals; (B) jungle : fauna; (C) countryside : cows; (D) orchard : trees; (E) vase : flowers
1985. B	1986. INDIGENOUS (A) foreign; (B) destitute; (C) insulting; (D) livid
2094. B	2095. DEMOTIC (A) tyrannical; (B) mobile; (C) selective; (D) fiendish

14. **B**	**15. ACOUSTIC** (A) culmination; (B) auditory; (C) acid forming; (D) feat
124. **A**	**125. CREDIBLE** (A) believable; (B) unbelievable; (C) correct; (D) suitable
234. **E**	**235. HABITAT** (A) routine; (B) carriage; (C) long-term resident; (D) dwelling place; (E) article of clothing
344. **C**	**345. PLIANT** (A) adhesive; (B) obdurate; (C) cringing; (D) flexible
454. **D**	**455. TANGENT** (A) touching; (B) parallel; (C) intersecting; (D) congruent
564. **D**	**565. ARGOT** (A) medicinal root; (B) wooden shoe; (C) jargon; (D) semi-precious stone
674. **A**	**675. CICERONE** (A) orator; (B) guide; (C) buffoon; (D) cavalier
784. **C**	**785. EPHEMERAL** (A) frightening; (B) weak; (C) transient; (D) ethereal
894. **A**	**895. HUMANITIES** (A) behaviorism; (B) treatment of human beings; (C) ancient classics; (D) social welfare
1004. **B**	**1005. MISCREANT** (A) victim; (B) misunderstood person; (C) scoundrel; (D) mistaken

1114. **B**	**1115. PREDATORY** (A) feline; (B) destructive; (C) prowling; (D) brutish
1223. **D**	**1224. STIPEND** (A) stipulation; (B) compensation; (C) strong odor; (D) difficult task
1332. **B**	**1333. ARACHNOID** (A) ornamented in fanciful style; (B) resembling a spider's web; (C) pertaining to Semitic languages; (D) curved like an eagle's beak
1441. **C**	**1442. FALDERAL** (A) descent; (B) nonsense; (C) leaf; (D) arrangement
1550. **B**	**1551. NESTORIAN** (A) harmful; (B) wise; (C) stupid; (D) loving; (E) utopian
1659. **A**	**1660. SLOE** (A) dark-purple fruit; (B) slow moving mammal; (C) rigged vessel; (D) cranberry bog
1768. **D**	**1769. COKE is to COAL as BREAD is to** (A) eat; (B) money; (C) dough; (D) man; (E) yeast
1877. **D**	**1878. IGNORANCE : BOOKS : :** (A) study : learning; (B) school : teacher; (C) candy : store; (D) darkness : lamps; (E) publication : fame
1986. **A**	**1987. DESUETUDE** (A) spasmodic action; (B) languor induced by hot weather; (C) state of use; (D) harmlessness
2095. **C**	**2096. DISSIDENCE** (A) propinquity; (B) efflorescence; (C) dubiety; (D) concurrence

15. B	**16. ACQUIESCE** (A) provide; (B) share; (C) climb; (D) submit; (E) proceed
125. A	**126. CREDULITY** (A) prize; (B) feebleness; (C) balance; (D) laziness; (E) belief
235. D	**236. HARASS** (A) rave; (B) shelter; (C) pierce; (D) restrain; (E) torment
345. D	**346. PLIGHT** (A) departure; (B) weight; (C) conspiracy; (D) predicament; (E) stamp
455. A	**456. TAUNT** (A) jeer at; (B) tighten; (C) rescue; (D) interest; (E) ward off
565. C	**566. ARRAIGN** (A) imprison; (B) straighten; (C) accuse; (D) confess
675. B	**676. CIRCUMSCRIBE** (A) correspond widely; (B) limit; (C) involve; (D) take a devious route
785. C	**786. EPITHET** (A) application; (B) figure of speech; (C) circumlocution; (D) appellative
895. C	**896. HUSBANDRY** (A) affection for spouse; (B) thrift; (C) virility; (D) uxoriousness
1005. C	**1006. MITIGATE** (A) attack; (B) alleviate; (C) mediate; (D) aggravate

1115. B	**1116. PREDILECTION** (A) preference; (B) prophecy; (C) foretaste; (D) predicate
1224. B	**1225. STRIATED** (A) straddled; (B) grooved; (C) weakened; (D) spotted
1333. B	**1334. ASKANT** (A) querulous; (B) requesting; (C) sloping; (D) meagre; (E) sidewise
1442. B	**1443. FANFARONADE** (A) Spanish dance; (B) mockery; (C) caprice; (D) delusion; (E) arrogant talk
1551. B	**1552. NEWEL** (A) prawn; (B) threshold; (C) acolyte; (D) principal post
1660. A	**1661. SOIREE** (A) a fond farewell; (B) an evening party; (C) skirtlike garment; (D) table service
1769. C	**1770. INDIAN is to AMERICA as HINDU is to** (A) Hindustan; (B) Mexico; (C) soil; (D) magic; (E) India
1878. D	**1879. AILMENT : DOCTOR : :** (A) medicine : pharmacist; (B) care : relief; (C) victim : crime; (D) fire : water; (E) war : victory
1987. C	**1988. MATUTINAL** (A) growing and developing steadily; (B) pertaining to the evening; (C) pertaining to the afternoon; (D) regularly established as an annual event
2096. D	**2097. DIVAGATION** (A) operatic solo; (B) adherence to topic; (C) underwater study; (D) summer travel

16. D	17. ACQUIT (A) increase; (B) harden; (C) clear; (D) sharpen; (E) sentence
126. E	127. CRUCIAL (A) technical; (B) decisive; (C) ill-natured; (D) inelegant; (E) greatly distorted
236. E	237. HUCKSTER (A) employer; (B) berry; (C) peddler; (D) color
346. D	347. PODIATRIST is one who treats ailments of (A) head; (B) infants; (C) feet; (D) adults
456. A	457. TEMPERANCE (A) moderation; (B) climate; (C) carelessness; (D) disagreeableness; (E) rigidity
566. C	567. ARRANT (A) shameless; (B) cowardly; (C) fleeing; (D) roving
676. B	677. CIRCUMSPECT (A) curious; (B) visionary; (C) cautious; (D) broadminded
786. D	787. EPITOME (A) effort; (B) summary; (C) struggle; (D) height
896. B	897. HUSTINGS (A) military expeditions; (B) waste material of textile mills; (C) inferior paintings; (D) electioneering platform
1006. B	1007. MNEMONIC (A) assisting memory; (B) concerning the theatre; (C) pertaining to motion; (D) pertaining to sound

1116. A	1117. PRESCIENCE (A) instinct; (B) foresight; (C) memory; (D) reason
1225. B	1226. STRIDULENT (A) grating; (B) acidulous; (C) vituperative; (D) swaggering
1334. E	1335. ASYNDETON (A) lacking parallelism; (B) periodic in structure; (C) faulty in conclusion; (D) omission of conjunctions; (E) contrary viewpoint
1443. E	1444. FARINACEOUS (A) mealy; (B) remote; (C) rock-like; (D) waxy
1552. D	1553. NEXUS (A) bond; (B) crux; (C) epitome; (D) aggregation
1661. B	1662. SONSY (A) sleepy; (B) loyal; (C) tipsy; (D) vain; (E) comely
1770. E	1771. WEALTH is to MERCENARY as GOLD is to (A) Midas; (B) miner; (C) fame; (D) eleemosynary; (E) South Africa
1879. D	1880. RETREAT : DEFEAT : : (A) retrench : depression; (B) victory : charge; (C) campaign : advance; (D) armistice : surrender; (E) stand : death
1988. B	1989. ABSOLVE (A) bless; (B) blame; (C) melt; (D) repent
2097. B	2098. EPIDEICTIC (A) modest; (B) concise; (C) intended to edify; (D) concentrated upon

17. **C**	**18. ACRID** (A) agricultural; (B) athletic; (C) extremely tasty; (D) fierce; (E) bitterly irritating
127. **B**	**128. CRYPTIC** (A) overt; (B) burned; (C) secret; (D) adroit
237. **C**	**238. HUMDRUM** (A) monotonous; (B) noisy; (C) misleading; (D) distinguished; (E) moist
347. **C**	**348. POMP** (A) magnificence; (B) aid; (C) thoughtfulness; (D) timeliness; (E) scarcity
457. **A**	**458. TEMPESTUOUS** (A) violent; (B) short-lived; (C) hard-hearted; (D) heated; (E) outrageous
567. **A**	**568. ARROGATE** (A) insult; (B) disparage; (C) usurp; (D) resign
677. **C**	**678. CLICHÉ** (A) idiom; (B) proverb; (C) much-used expression; (D) precipice
787. **B**	**788. EQUITY** (A) fairness; (B) distribution; (C) injustice; (D) consideration
897. **D**	**898. HYPERBOLE** (A) exaggeration; (B) plane curve; (C) onomatopoeia; (D) assumption
1007. **A**	**1008. MOIETY** (A) large majority; (B) aggregate; (C) tenderness; (D) about half

1117. B	1118. PRESENTIMENT (A) indictment; (B) foreboding; (C) sympathy; (D) gift
1226. A	1227. STULTIFY (A) make foolish; (B) stun; (C) inhibit; (D) render helpless
1335. D	1336. ATELIER (A) studio; (B) winged messenger; (C) prophet; (D) unit of measure
1444. A	1445. FARRAGO (A) mixture; (B) dance step; (C) failure; (D) ill-tempered woman
1553. A	1554. NICTITATE (A) build a nest; (B) use tobacco excessively; (C) wink; (D) neigh
1662. E	1663. SORICINE (A) related to witchcraft; (B) shrewlike; (C) greedy; (D) syllogistic
1771. A	1772. BOTTLE is to BRITTLE as TIRE is to (A) elastic; (B) scarce; (C) rubber; (D) spheroid; (E) automobile
1880. A	1881. OBLITERATE : PAINT : : (A) earthquake : city; (B) write : ink; (C) destroy : house; (D) drown : water; (E) artist : canvas
1989. B	1990. SACROSANCT (A) sacerdotal; (B) sanctimonious; (C) sacramental; (D) unholy
2098. A	2099. FARINACEOUS (A) mealy; (B) remote; (C) rock-like; (D) waxy

18. E	**19. ACUMEN** (A) beauty; (B) marked poise; (C) keen discernment; (D) illness
128. C	**129. CRYSTALLIZE** (A) overwhelm completely; (B) lead to confusion; (C) assume definite form; (D) blame; (E) glamorize
238. A	**239. HYPOTHETICAL** (A) magical; (B) visual; (C) two-faced; (D) theoretical; (E) excitable
348. A	**349. POMPOUS** (A) occasionally leaky; (B) self-important; (C) thoughtful; (D) powerful; (E) respectful
458. A	**459. TENACITY** (A) firmness; (B) sagacity; (C) temerity; (D) thinness
568. C	**569. ARROYO** (A) ranch; (B) cliff; (C) gully; (D) cactus
678. C	**679. CLOTURE** (A) caucus; (B) filibuster; (C) closing; (D) roll-call
788. A	**789. EQUIVOCAL** (A) corresponding; (B) hidden; (C) uncertain; (D) average
898. A	**899. IDYLLIC** (A) pastoral; (B) reverent; (C) sophisticated; (D) slothful
1008. D	**1009. MOLLIFY** (A) tremble; (B) appease; (C) aggravate; (D) mutter

1118. B	**1119. PRETENTIOUS** (A) seeking advantage; (B) ostentatious; (C) grasping; (D) given to making excuses
1227. A	**1228. SUBLIMINAL** (A) exalted; (B) vicarious; (C) subconscious; (D) redirected
1336. A	**1337. ATHANASIA** (A) mercy killing; (B) sleeplessness; (C) euphoria; (D) immortality
1445. A	**1446. FERVID** (A) ardent; (B) charitable; (C) gay; (D) savage; (E) untamed
1554. C	**1555. NIDUS** (A) negation; (B) knitting; (C) nest; (D) lid
1663. B	**1664. SOUGH** (A) sigh; (B) refulgence; (C) lint; (D) erosion
1772. A	**1773. PENINSULA is to LAND as BAY is to** (A) boats; (B) pay; (C) ocean; (D) Massachusetts
1881. B	**1882. SYMPATHY : PROTAGONIST : :** (A) hate : villain; (B) cry : misfortune; (C) love : store; (D) hero : affection; (E) sadness : pity
1990. D	**1991. POLEMIC** (A) arctic; (B) electro-chemical; (C) agreeable; (D) statistical
2099. C	**2100. FLACON** (A) pennant; (B) slender leaf; (C) flaming torch; (D) large bottle

19. **C**	**20. ADAGE** (A) proverb; (B) supplement; (C) tool; (D) youth; (E) hardness
129. **C**	**130. CULINARY** (A) having to do with cooking; (B) pertaining to dressmaking; (C) fond of eating; (D) loving money; (E) tending to be secretive
239. **D**	**240. ICONOCLAST** (A) idol; (B) assailant; (C) invest; (D) divest
349. **B**	**350. POSTDATED** (A) past date; (B) future date; (C) no date; (D) current date
459. **A**	**460. TENTATIVE** (A) formal; (B) experimental; (C) affectionate; (D) tight; (E) progressive
569. **C**	**570. ARTICULATION** (A) covenant; (B) maneuver; (C) aspiration; (D) enunciation
679. **C**	**680. CLOY** (A) glut; (B) cling; (C) mix; (D) sweeten
789. **C**	**790. EQUIVOCATE** (A) ride a horse; (B) balance; (C) mislead deliberately; (D) arbitrate
899. **A**	**900. IMBROGLIO** (A) harem; (B) difficult situation; (C) involved lie; (D) cameo
1009. **B**	**1010. MONAD** (A) single-voiced melody; (B) bacchante; (C) generative tissue; (D) simple organism

1119. B	**1120. PRIMA FACIE** (A) in the study of prime causes; (B) in an early stage; (C) on first appearance; (D) in the manner of a diva
1228. C	**1229. SUBSUME** (A) include; (B) conceal; (C) devour; (D) underestimate
1337. D	**1338. AURIFEROUS** (A) deafening; (B) odorous; (C) iron-bearing; (D) gold-bearing
1446. A	**1447. FESTINATE** (A) ardent; (B) morbid; (C) rankling; (D) hasten; (E) fertile
1555. C	**1556. NIRVANA** (A) loss of auditory acuity; (B) oblivion to external reality; (C) loss of courage; (D) muscular atrophy
1664. A	**1665. SPATE** (A) mollusk; (B) quarrel; (C) pause; (D) torrent
1773. C	**1774. HOUR is to MINUTE as MINUTE is to** (A) man; (B) week; (C) second; (D) short
1882. A	**1883. VICTORY : JUBILATION : :** (A) defeat : consternation; (B) graduation : congratulation; (C) election : celebration; (D) wedding : felicitation; (E) slavery : emancipation
1991. C	**1992. INTRANSIGENT** (A) impassable; (B) reconcilable; (C) harsh; (D) fly-by-night
2100. D	**2101. FROWARD** (A) offensive; (B) perverse; (C) progressive; (D) tractable

20. **A**	**21. ADEPT** (A) grateful; (B) additional; (C) awkward; (D) skillful; (E) orderly
130. **A**	**131. CULMINATION** (A) rebellion; (B) lighting system; (C) climax; (D) destruction; (E) mystery
240. **B**	**241. IGNOMINY** (A) illiteracy; (B) ill luck; (C) disgrace; (D) despair
350. **B**	**351. POSTERITY** (A) ancestors; (B) ownership; (C) amendment; (D) descendants; (E) fellow-citizens
460. **B**	**461. TENUOUS** (A) coarse; (B) term of office; (C) slender; (D) end of the line
570. **D**	**571. ARTIFACT** (A) product of human workmanship; (B) stratagem; (C) duplication; (D) artful or skillful contrivance
680. **A**	**681. COERCE** (A) persuade; (B) compel; (C) agree; (D) douse
790. **C**	**791. ERUDITE** (A) scholarly; (B) impolite; (C) dignified; (D) concealed
900. **B**	**901. IMMANENT** (A) impending; (B) inherent; (C) machine-made; (D) renowned
1010. **D**	**1011. MONITION** (A) presentiment; (B) currency; (C) caution; (D) armament

1120. C	**1121. PRIMORDIAL** (A) first-born; (B) slimy; (C) rudimentary; (D) obsolescent
1229. A	**1230. SUBTERFUGE** (A) volcanic ash; (B) irony; (C) hidden fear; (D) evasion
1338. D	**1339. AUSCULTATION** (A) listening; (B) repetition; (C) divination; (D) conference
1447. D	**1448. FETID** (A) hot; (B) damp; (C) noisome; (D) decayed
1556. B	**1557. OBI** (A) movement showing courtesy; (B) broad sash worn around the waist; (C) mark used in ancient manuscripts; (D) mammal related to the giraffe
1665. D	**1666. SPLAYED** (A) hunched; (B) spread out; (C) splashed; (D) knobby
1774. C	**1775. ABIDE is to DEPART as STAY is to** (A) over; (B) home; (C) play; (D) leave
1883. C	**1884. MONOTONY : BOREDOM : :** (A) perseverance : success; (B) factory : salary; (C) automation : saving; (D) interest : complication; (E) repetition : indolence
1992. B	**1993. INGENUOUS** (A) quick; (B) mischievous; (C) talented; (D) plotting
2101. D	**2102. HALIDOM** (A) fief; (B) martyrdom; (C) ancestry; (D) ungodliness

21. D	**22. ADHERENT** (A) confessor; (B) witness; (C) judge; (D) interceptor; (E) follower
131. C	**132. CURTAIL** (A) jump; (B) lessen; (C) design; (D) collect; (E) dance
241. C	**242. ILLICIT** (A) unlawful; (B) overpowering; (C) ill-advised; (D) small-scale; (E) unreadable
351. D	**352. PRECARIOUS** (A) foresighted; (B) careful; (C) modest; (D) headstrong; (E) uncertain
461. C	**462. TEPID** (A) hesitant; (B) fierce; (C) lukewarm; (D) singular; (E) temperamental
571. A	**572. ARTIFICER** (A) mimic; (B) artistic worker; (C) copyist of works of art; (D) curator
681. B	**682. COGENT** (A) geared; (B) incurring liability; (C) persuasive; (D) allied
791. A	**792. ESCHEW** (A) copy; (B) digest; (C) avoid; (D) despise
901. B	**902. IMMINENT** (A) sudden; (B) important; (C) delayed; (D) threatening; (E) forceful
1011. C	**1012. MOPPET** (A) small floor mop; (B) rag doll; (C) spindling tree; (D) musical term

1121. C	1122. PRISTINE (A) bright; (B) primitive; (C) proper; (D) haughty
1230. D	1231. SUPERSONIC (A) greater than the speed of sound; (B) faster than lightning; (C) atomic-powered; (D) higher than the atmosphere
1339. A	1340. AUSTRAL (A) starry; (B) southern; (C) Australian; (D) austere
1448. C	1449. FLACON (A) slender leaf; (B) pennant; (C) flaming torch; (D) small bottle
1557. B	1558. OBJURGATE (A) forswear; (B) appeal; (C) upbraid; (D) importune
1666. B	1667. SPOOR (A) mutation; (B) trail of wild animal; (C) unicellular reproductive body; (D) fetid odor
1775. D	1776. JANUARY is to FEBRUARY as JUNE is to (A) July; (B) May; (C) month; (D) year
1884. A	1885. CONDONE : TREACHERY : : (A) punish : criminal; (B) mitigate : penitence; (C) overlook : aberrations; (D) mistake : judgment; (E) ignore : loyalty
1993. D	1994. CANARD (A) rebus; (B) true story; (C) scurrilous publication; (D) flattery
2102. D	2103. IMMURED (A) guaranteed; (B) free; (C) iniquitous; (D) suffered

22. E	**23. ADROIT** (A) aimless; (B) clever; (C) moist; (D) false; (E) nearby
132. B	**133. CUSTODY** (A) dessert; (B) plea for action; (C) swearing; (D) imprisonment; (E) regard
242. A	**243. IMMORTAL** (A) disgraceful; (B) stupendous; (C) steadfast; (D) blameless; (E) imperishable
352. E	**353. PRECEDENCE** (A) procession; (B) impulsiveness; (C) formality; (D) priority; (E) hesitation
462. C	**463. TERSELY** (A) vigorously; (B) with difficulty; (C) informally; (D) physically; (E) concisely
572. B	**573. ASCETIC** (A) self-denying; (B) acrimonious; (C) exclusive; (D) fragrant
682. C	**683. COGNOMEN** (A) surname; (B) machine part; (C) misnomer; (D) oddity
792. C	**793. EULOGIZE** (A) decry bitterly; (B) write skillfully; (C) praise highly; (D) admonish sternly
902. D	**903. IMMOLATE** (A) render immortal; (B) make a martyr of; (C) imprison; (D) sacrifice
1012. B	**1013. MORBID** (A) deceased; (B) unhealthy; (C) flowering; (D) fettered

1122. B	**1123. PROBITY** (A) likelihood; (B) curiosity; (C) proximity; (D) integrity
1231. A	**1232. SUPPOSITITIOUS** (A) defensible; (B) vengeful; (C) spurious; (D) magical
1340. B	**1341. AUTOCHTHONOUS** (A) independent; (B) self-sufficient; (C) indigenous; (D) unattached
1449. D	**1450. FORENSIC** (A) prohibiting; (B) argumentative; (C) oral; (D) fluent
1558. C	**1559. OBTURATION** (A) closing; (B) irreconcilability; (C) stubbornness; (D) eulogy
1667. B	**1668. STERTOROUSNESS** (A) mercurial temper; (B) heavy snoring; (C) blowiness; (D) reverberating tones
1776. A	**1777. BOLD is to TIMID as ADVANCE is to** (A) proceed; (B) retreat; (C) campaign; (D) soldiers
1885. C	**1886. POWER : BATTERY : :** (A) vitamins : metabolism; (B) exercise : strength; (C) recuperation : convalescence; (D) automobile : engine; (E) light : kerosene
1994. B	**1995. DISINTERESTED** (A) opposed; (B) contemptuous; (C) superficial; (D) partial
2103. B	**2104. INAMORATA** (A) nameless person; (B) enemy; (C) assumed name; (D) lovelorn person

23. B	**24. ADVENT** (A) attachment; (B) reference; (C) arrival; (D) excitement; (E) complaint
133. D	**134. DEADLOCK** (A) useless material; (B) fatigue; (C) will; (D) fixed limit; (E) state of inaction
243. E	**244. IMMUNITY** (A) disease; (B) publicity; (C) mercy; (D) changeableness; (E) freedom
353. D	**354. PRECEDENT** (A) preferment; (B) result; (C) preceding instance; (D) prestige
463. E	**464. THWART** (A) assist; (B) whimper; (C) slice; (D) escape; (E) block
573. A	**574. ASPERITY** (A) acrimony; (B) lack of sincerity; (C) lack of realism; (D) ambition
683. A	**684. COLANDER** (A) species of lizard; (B) upright of a sluice; (C) baking dish; (D) vessel perforated for use as a sieve or strainer
793. C	**794. EUPHEMISM** (A) affected style; (B) belief in perfectibility; (C) inoffensive turn of phrase; (D) profane remark
903. D	**904. IMMURE** (A) ossify; (B) enclose; (C) fertilize; (D) inhere
1013. B	**1014. MORDANT** (A) biting; (B) deathly; (C) plastic; (D) multiplying

1123. D	**1124. PROCLIVITY** (A) propensity; (B) rapid descent; (C) devoted adherence; (D) buoyancy
1232. C	**1233. SURCEASE** (A) sweetness; (B) resignation; (C) end; (D) hope
1341. C	**1342. AVATAR** (A) throw-back; (B) incantation; (C) incarnation; (D) immolation
1450. B	**1451. FORTUITISM** (A) premeditation; (B) gigantism; (C) opportunism; (D) philosophy of chance
1559. A	**1560. OCHLOCRACY** (A) government by ukase; (B) army rule; (C) mob rule; (D) government by the select few
1668. B	**1669. STIGMATA** (A) stems; (B) marks; (C) suggestions; (D) stimuli; (E) false modesty
1777. B	**1778. ABOVE is to BELOW as TOP is to** (A) spin; (B) bottom; (C) surface; (D) side
1886. E	**1887. DEPRESSION : UNEMPLOYMENT : :** (A) capital : interest; (B) legislation : lobbying; (C) emaciation : debilitation; (D) deterioration : rust; (E) recession : inefficiency
1995. D	**1996. PROPITIATE** (A) anger; (B) approach; (C) predict; (D) applaud
2104. D	**2105. INSPISSATED** (A) animated; (B) thickened; (C) attenuated; (D) mixed thoroughly

24. C	**25. AGENDA** (A) receipt; (B) agent; (C) combination; (D) memoranda
134. E	**135. DEARTH** (A) scarcity; (B) width; (C) affection; (D) wealth; (E) warmth
244. E	**245. IMPAIR** (A) consume; (B) control; (C) design; (D) damage; (E) restrain
354. C	**355. PRECIPICE** (A) forecast; (B) cliff; (C) danger; (D) instructor; (E) obstinacy
464. E	**465. TIMBRE** (A) wood; (B) fear; (C) timing; (D) tone
574. A	**575. ASPERSION** (A) deflation; (B) routing; (C) denial; (D) defamation
684. D	**685. COMATOSE** (A) unconscious; (B) disheveled; (C) reserved; (D) obstinate
794. C	**795. EUPHEMISTIC** (A) having good digestion; (B) less offensive in phrasing; (C) exhibiting great enjoyment; (D) excessively elegant in style
904. B	**905. IMPASSIVE** (A) active; (B) apathetic; (C) determined; (D) reluctant
1014. A	**1015. MORIBUND** (A) vexatious; (B) biting; (C) dying; (D) sullen

1124. A	**1125. PROFLIGATE** (A) sadistic; (B) dissolute; (C) magnanimous; (D) bumptious
1233. C	**1234. SURREPTITIOUS** (A) scandalous; (B) evil; (C) clandestine; (D) stupefying
1342. C	**1343. BALDRIC** (A) coat; (B) vest; (C) belt; (D) cape
1451. D	**1452. FRANKLIN** (A) merchant; (B) freeholder; (C) English archer; (D) seller of pardons
1560. C	**1561. OGIVE** (A) leader; (B) arch; (C) prestidigitation; (D) benediction
1669. B	**1670. STINT** (A) reward; (B) wonder; (C) demand; (D) limitation; (E) cure
1778. B	**1779. LION is to ANIMAL as ROSE is to** (A) smell; (B) leaf; (C) plant; (D) thorn
1887. D	**1888. DIETING : OVERWEIGHT : :** (A) overeating : gluttony; (B) poverty : sickness; (C) gourmet : underweight; (D) doctor : arthritis; (E) exercise : weakness
1996. A	**1997. MURRAIN** (A) marshland; (B) blessing; (C) glacial ridge; (D) land held inalienably
2105. C	**2106. INTERPELLATE** (A) alter by inserting; (B) clarify; (C) admonish; (D) answer informally

25. **D**	**26. AGGRAVATE** (A) accuse; (B) consider; (C) grieve; (D) intensify; (E) engrave
135. **A**	**136. DECADENCE** (A) ten-sided; (B) ten-year period; (C) rare; (D) decay
245. **D**	**246. IMPARTIAL** (A) favorite; (B) just; (C) selfish; (D) difficult; (E) meaningless
355. **B**	**356. PRECOCIOUS** (A) valuable; (B) steep; (C) mentally accelerated; (D) delicate
465. **D**	**466. TORPOR** (A) tropical storm; (B) numbness; (C) destroyer; (D) surface features
575. **D**	**576. ASSEVERATE** (A) appoint; (B) affirm; (C) slice; (D) disagree
685. **A**	**686. COMITY** (A) solace; (B) beauty; (C) union; (D) courtesy
795. **B**	**796. EUPHORIA** (A) sense of well-being; (B) assumption of friendliness; (C) ability to speak well; (D) eagerness to agree
905. **B**	**906. IMPEACH** (A) accuse; (B) judge; (C) find guilty; (D) remove
1015. **C**	**1016. MORPHOLOGICAL** (A) the effects of a sedative; (B) form and structure; (C) the scientific study of sleep; (D) thought processes while dreaming

1125. B	**1126. PROGNATHOUS** (A) degenerate; (B) diagnostic; (C) having projecting jaws; (D) prehuman
1234. C	**1235. SURROGATE** (A) will; (B) substitute; (C) court clerk; (D) criminal court
1343. C	**1344. BASALT** (A) marble; (B) granite; (C) chemical; (D) crystal
1452. B	**1453. FRENUM** (A) membrane; (B) state of anger; (C) tributary; (D) gratuity
1561. B	**1562. ONEIROMANCY** (A) divination by dreams; (B) astrology; (C) fortune-telling by cards; (D) phrenology
1670. D	**1671. STRABISMUS** (A) transplanted retina; (B) glaucoma; (C) cataract; (D) cross-eye
1779. C	**1780. TIGER is to CARNIVOROUS as HORSE is to** (A) cow; (B) pony; (C) buggy; (D) herbivorous
1888. E	**1889. STREPTOCOCCI : PNEUMONIA : :** (A) boat : trip; (B) quinine : malaria; (C) cause : sickness; (D) malnutrition : beriberi; (E) medicine : sickness
1997. B	**1998. FERAL** (A) iron-bearing; (B) panel; (C) calm; (D) violent
2106. D	**2107. JARDINIERE** (A) professional soldier; (B) small flowerpot; (C) female gardener; (D) beekeeper

26. **D**	**27. AGHAST** (A) eager; (B) farmer; (C) intense; (D) frightened
136. **D**	**137. DEFER** (A) discourage; (B) postpone; (C) empty; (D) minimize; (E) estimate
246. **B**	**247. IMPEDIMENT** (A) rostrum; (B) table; (C) difficulty; (D) pseudopod
356. **C**	**357. PREDATORY** (A) introductory; (B) intellectual; (C) preaching; (D) robbing
466. **B**	**467. TORTUOUS** (A) collapsed; (B) burning; (C) twisted; (D) laborious
576. **B**	**577. ASSEVERATION** (A) separation; (B) compensation; (C) retention; (D) assertion
686. **D**	**687. COMMODIOUS** (A) fashionable; (B) complaisant; (C) spacious; (D) of similar origin
796. **A**	**797. EVINCE** (A) dominate; (B) persuade; (C) defeat; (D) manifest
906. **A**	**907. IMPECCABLE** (A) impecunious; (B) neat; (C) flawless; (D) unspeakable
1016. **B**	**1017. MOTLEY** (A) vulgar; (B) heterogeneous; (C) crowded; (D) forest green

1126. **C**	**1127. PROLIX** (A) anticipative; (B) generative; (C) verbose; (D) prophylactic
1235. **E**	**1236. SYCOPHANTIC** (A) uxorious; (B) voluptuous; (C) parasitic; (D) significant
1344. **A**	**1345. BASILIC** (A) deadly; (B) fundamental; (C) slaggy; (D) kingly
1453. **A**	**1454. FRISEUR** (A) cook; (B) hairdresser; (C) fraud; (D) freezer
1562. **A**	**1563. OPT** (A) grant; (B) perform; (C) choose; (D) discern
1671. **D**	**1672. STRICTURE** (A) adverse criticism; (B) harsh demand; (C) precise description; (D) critical situation
1780. **D**	**1781. SAILOR is to NAVY as SOLDIER is to** (A) gun; (B) cap; (C) hill; (D) army
1889. **D**	**1890. NAIVE : CHEAT : :** (A) sensible : successful; (B) retaliate : hurt; (C) gullible : convince; (D) contentious : scorn; (E) simple : win
1998. **C**	**1999. SOMATIC** (A) sleepy; (B) spiritual; (C) seminal; (D) body
2107. **B**	**2108. LENITIVE** (A) shortening; (B) emollient; (C) painful; (D) elongating

27. D	**28. AGILITY** (A) wisdom; (B) nimbleness; (C) agreeable; (D) simplicity; (E) excitement
137. B	**138. DEFRAUD** (A) cheat; (B) uncover; (C) pay; (D) delay; (E) accuse
247. C	**248. IMPERTURBABLE** (A) quick-tempered; (B) calm; (C) envious; (D) excitable; (E) impassable
357. D	**358. PREROGATIVE** (A) privilege; (B) inferiority; (C) redemption; (D) naval command; (E) combination
467. C	**468. TRANQUIL** (A) restless; (B) calm; (C) weary; (D) understanding; (E) blooming
577. D	**578. ASSUAGE** (A) purge; (B) ease; (C) sicken; (D) aggravate
687. C	**688. COMPENDIOUS** (A) concise; (B) heavy; (C) learned; (D) pending
797. D	**798. EWER** (A) pitcher; (B) metal pin; (C) tender of sheep; (D) wood craftsman
907. C	**908. IMPECUNIOUS** (A) stingy; (B) poor; (C) fastidious; (D) blameless
1017. B	**1018. MOUNTEBANK** (A) barker; (B) pickpocket; (C) peak; (D) charlatan

1127. C	1128. PROPENSITY (A) inclination; (B) forethought; (C) quickness to anger; (D) thoughtfulness
1236. C	1237. SYNCOPE (A) swoon; (B) council; (C) grammar; (D) symptom
1345. D	1346. BASSET (A) wicker cradle; (B) woodwind instrument; (C) short-legged hound; (D) dragnet
1454. B	1455. FUSTIAN (A) confusion; (B) fine silk; (C) bombast; (D) unnecessary activity
1563. C	1564. ORGANON (A) a complex structure; (B) genesis; (C) method; (D) any living being
1672. A	1673. STRIDULOUS (A) galloping; (B) impatient; (C) snobbish; (D) shrill-sounding
1781. D	1782. PICTURE is to SEE as SOUND is to (A) noise; (B) music; (C) hear; (D) bark
1890. C	1891. ERRORS : INEXPERIENCE : : (A) costly : mistakes; (B) training : economical; (C) news : publication; (D) success : victory; (E) thefts : carelessness
1999. B	2000. INELUCTABLE (A) avoidable; (B) inscrutable; (C) approachable; (D) esoteric
2108. C	2109. LITIGIOUS (A) ornate in literary style; (B) illegally threatening; (C) agreeable; (D) close to the shoreline

28. B	**29. ALIMENT** (A) illness; (B) intestine; (C) food; (D) acidity
138. A	**139. DEFT** (A) skillful; (B) wise; (C) particular; (D) awkward; (E) disagreeable
248. B	**249. IMPERVIOUS** (A) arrogant; (B) officious; (C) impulsive; (D) impenetrable
358. A	**359. PRESTIGE** (A) speed; (B) influence; (C) omen; (D) pride; (E) excuse
468. B	**469. TRENCHANT** (A) forceful; (B) triangular; (C) longing; (D) tricky
578. B	**579. ASTUTE** (A) sagacious; (B) austere; (C) astounding; (D) stolid
688. A	**689. COMPENDIUM** (A) volume; (B) platform; (C) enlargement; (D) epitome
798. A	**799. EXACERBATE** (A) aggravate; (B) unearth; (C) punish; (D) refine
908. B	**909. IMPERIOUS** (A) resistant; (B) arrogant; (C) irascible; (D) defective
1018. D	**1019. MULCT** (A) deprive; (B) abscond; (C) pluck; (D) unearth

1128. A	1129. **PROPINQUITY** (A) good fortune; (B) proximity; (C) proof; (D) sharp movement
1237. A	1238. **TANTAMOUNT** (A) superior; (B) related; (C) equivalent; (D) due
1346. C	1347. **BATTEN** (A) gather; (B) seize; (C) fatten; (D) shatter
1455. C	1456. **GAFFER** (A) ship's spar; (B) gossip; (C) aged rustic; (D) bargain
1564. C	1565. **ORIEL** (A) sprite; (B) kind of window; (C) buttress; (D) song bird
1673. D	1674. **STROBIC** (A) pausing; (B) whirling; (C) toothed; (D) cosmic; (E) reverberating tones
1782. C	1783. **SUCCESS is to JOY as FAILURE is to** (A) sadness; (B) success; (C) fail; (D) work
1891. E	1892. **FORECAST : HAPPENING : :** (A) prophecy : miracle; (B) analyze : problem; (C) exculpate : criminal; (D) premonition : disaster; (E) elucidate : explanation
2000. A	2001. **FROWARD** (A) complaisant; (B) cooperative; (C) candid; (D) precocious
2109. C	2110. **LUBRICOUS** (A) mercenary; (B) rough; (C) tubular; (D) thrifty

29. C	**30. ALLOCATE** (A) address; (B) tempt; (C) distribute; (D) permit; (E) drift
139. A	**140. DEHYDRATED** (A) airless; (B) worthless; (C) waterless; (D) pointless
249. D	**250. IMPETUOUS** (A) faultless; (B) masterful; (C) insolent; (D) urgent; (E) hasty
359. B	**360. PRESUMPTUOUS** (A) forward; (B) foreshadowing; (C) costly; (D) renewable; (E) unhealthful
469. A	**470. TRITE** (A) brilliant; (B) unusual; (C) funny; (D) stiff; (E) commonplace
579. A	**580. ATAVISM** (A) reversion to type; (B) political favoritism; (C) inclination to cruelty; (D) basic life force
689. D	**690. COMPLAISANT** (A) discontented; (B) smug; (C) obliging; (D) satisfied
799. A	**800. EXCEPTIONABLE** (A) not better than average; (B) objectionable; (C) out of the ordinary; (D) captious
909. B	**910. IMPINGE** (A) pawn; (B) fatten up; (C) encroach upon; (D) stab
1019. A	**1020. MUNIFICENT** (A) bountiful; (B) plentiful; (C) powerful; (D) splendid

1129. B	**1130. PROPITIATE** (A) placate; (B) approach; (C) predict; (D) applaud
1238. C	**1239. TAUTOLOGICAL** (A) extreme; (B) laconic; (C) fallacious; (D) repetitious
1347. C	**1348. BELAY** (A) disclaim; (B) secure; (C) obligate; (D) burden
1456. C	**1457. GALLIMAUFRY** (A) hodgepodge; (B) omelet; (C) harness; (D) equipage
1565. B	**1566. ORISON** (A) prayer; (B) constellation south of Gemini; (C) ensign or standard; (D) aperture
1674. B	**1675. SUBORN** (A) inferior; (B) confidential; (C) bribe; (D) append
1783. A	**1784. HOPE is to DESPAIR as HAPPINESS is to** (A) frolic; (B) fun; (C) joy; (D) sadness
1892. B	**1893. CAT : FELINE : :** (A) horse : equine; (B) tiger : carnivorous; (C) bird : vulpine; (D) chair : furniture; (E) sit : recline
2001. B	**2002. SIMPER** (A) sniff; (B) frown; (C) sob; (D) smile
2110. B	**2111. LUCUBRATE** (A) write stupidly; (B) whine incessantly; (C) sail nearer the wind; (D) remove friction

30. C	31. ALOOF (A) hard; (B) imaginary; (C) reserved; (D) happy; (E) willing
140. C	141. DEITY (A) renown; (B) divinity; (C) delicacy; (D) destiny; (E) futility
250. E	251. IMPLICATE (A) please; (B) expect; (C) involve; (D) trick; (E) ambush
360. A	361. PRETEXT (A) argument; (B) excuse; (C) preliminary examination; (D) first glimpse; (E) sermon
470. E	471. TRYST (A) meeting; (B) trick; (C) drama; (D) trifle
580. A	581. ATAVISTIC (A) overeager; (B) narrow-minded; (C) reverting to a primitive type; (D) pertaining to an uncle
690. C	691. COMPLIANT (A) self-satisfied; (B) religious; (C) obedient; (D) devious
800. B	801. EXCORIATE (A) rack; (B) expel; (C) disembarrass; (D) flay
910. C	911. IMPIOUS (A) rash; (B) mischievous; (C) irreverent; (D) indecent
1020. A	1021. MURRAIN (A) marsh land; (B) plague; (C) glacial ridge; (D) land held inalienably

1130. **A**	**1131. PROPITIOUS** (A) auspicious; (B) reliable; (C) cheerful; (D) tempting
1239. **D**	**1240. TAWDRY** (A) cheap and gaudy; (B) obscene; (C) reddish brown; (D) worthless
1348. **B**	**1349. BELDAM** (A) hag; (B) clamor; (C) gossip; (D) princess; (E) attendant
1457. **A**	**1458. GAMBIT** (A) wager; (B) stirrup; (C) frolic; (D) exchange
1566. **A**	**1567. OSIER** (A) inhabitant of Indiana; (B) any large bone; (C) willow with twigs flexible enough for wickerwork; (D) poplar
1675. **C**	**1676. SUFFRAGAN** (A) assistant; (B) franchise; (C) voter; (D) hardship
1784. **D**	**1785. PRETTY is to UGLY as ATTRACT is to** (A) fine; (B) repel; (C) nice; (D) draw
1893. **A**	**1894. ADVERSITY : HAPPINESS : :** (A) fear : misfortune; (B) troublesome : petulance; (C) vehemence : serenity; (D) solace : adversity; (E) graduation : felicitation
2002. **D**	**2003. REDOUBT** (A) homestead; (B) weakness; (C) supply dump; (D) sanctuary
2111. **A** *Page 62*	**2112. MEGACEPHALY** (A) smallness of head; (B) magnification of vision; (C) malformation of feet; (D) inordinate loss of hair

31. C	32. AMBIGUITY (A) adherence; (B) affliction; (C) aspiration; (D) doubtfulness
141. B	142. DELUGE (A) deceive; (B) follow; (C) conclude; (D) transport; (E) overwhelm
251. C	252. IMPORT (A) security; (B) denial; (C) meaning; (D) mission; (E) injustice
361. B	362. PREVAIL (A) introduce; (B) misjudge; (C) rescue; (D) triumph; (E) overestimate
471. A	472. TURBULENCE (A) treachery; (B) commotion; (C) fear; (D) triumph; (E) overflow
581. C	582. ATROPHY (A) injury; (B) wasting away; (C) stanza of a ballad; (D) disaster
691. C	692. CONCATENATION (A) connection; (B) confusion; (C) terror; (D) loud report
801. D	802. EXCULPATE (A) avoid a commitment; (B) extract a confession; (C) absolve from guilt; (D) withdraw from a group
911. C	912. IMPLEMENT (A) plan together; (B) act hurriedly; (C) carry out; (D) give credit
1021. B	1022. NADIR (A) highest point; (B) opposite of zenith; (C) complete negation; (D) apex of a right triangle

1131. A	1132. PROROGUE
	(A) endow with privilege; (B) defer; (C) categorize; (D) ratiocinate

1240. A	1241. TEMERITY
	(A) fear; (B) equanimity; (C) deposition; (D) audacity

1349. A	1350. BESOM
	(A) wax; (B) broom; (C) hive; (D) bias; (E) breast

1458. D	1459. GAMMON
	(A) stake; (B) humbug; (C) major scale; (D) passage; (E) reproduction

1567. C	1568. OUTRÉ
	(A) bizarre; (B) chic; (C) subtle; (D) boycotted

1676. A	1677. SUPERNAL
	(A) lethargic; (B) heavenly; (C) credulous; (D) without drugs; (E) costly

1785. B	1786. PUPIL is to TEACHER as CHILD is to
	(A) parent; (B) dolly; (C) youngster; (D) obey

1894. C	1895. NECKLACE : ADORNMENT : :
	(A) medal : decoration; (B) bronze : medal; (C) window : house; (D) pearl : diamond; (E) scarf : dress

2003. B	2004. SALAD DAYS
	(A) days of one's babyhood; (B) days of yore; (C) days of wide experience; (D) halcyon days

2112. A	2113. MENDICITY
	(A) lying; (B) giving; (C) venerating; (D) repairing

32. D	**33. AMETHYST** (A) purplish; (B) fish; (C) friendly; (D) gelatin
142. E	**143. DEMEANOR** (A) bearing; (B) expenditure; (C) irritability; (D) questionnaire; (E) death
252. C	**253. INADVERTENTLY** (A) actually; (B) harmlessly; (C) heedlessly; (D) angrily; (E) confidently
362. D	**363. PREVALENT** (A) brilliant; (B) mediocre; (C) previous; (D) occurring often; (E) occurring seldom
472. B	**473. ULTIMATUM** (A) shrewd plan; (B) final terms; (C) first defeat; (D) dominant leader; (E) electric motor
582. B	**583. ATTAINDER** (A) transfer of a faulty title; (B) defendant's reply; (C) extinction of civil rights; (D) repossession of property
692. A	**693. CONDIGN** (A) pretentious; (B) patronizing; (C) pungent; (D) suitable
802. C	**803. EXECRATION** (A) curse; (B) atonement; (C) death; (D) hatred
912. C	**913. IMPRECATE** (A) involve; (B) curse; (C) promise; (D) betray
1022. B	**1023. N.B.** (A) bill of notary; (B) boxes nailed; (C) note well; (D) unbound

1132. **B**	**1133. PROSAIC** (A) didactic; (B) literary; (C) dull; (D) controversial
1241. **D**	**1242. TEMERARIOUS** (A) rash; (B) frightened; (C) quiet; (D) dangerous
1350. **B**	**1351. BIGHT** (A) cause of destruction; (B) loop; (C) knavery; (D) stagnant backwater
1459. **B**	**1460. GAZEBO** (A) knickknack; (B) bird watcher; (C) small deer; (D) summerhouse
1568. **A**	**1569. PALANQUIN** (A) litter borne by poles on men's shoulders; (B) knightly champion; (C) buffoon; (D) pyramidal building
1677. **B**	**1678. SUSURRANT** (A) murmuring; (B) crepitant; (C) lambent; (D) coruscating
1786. **A**	**1787. CITY is to MAYOR as ARMY is to** (A) navy; (B) soldier; (C) general; (D) private
1895. **A**	**1896. GUN : HOLSTER : :** (A) shoe : soldier; (B) sword : warrior; (C) ink : pen; (D) shoot : carry; (E) cannon : plunder
2004. **C**	**2005. CALUMNIOUS** (A) disastrous; (B) conspiratorial; (C) querulous; (D) complimenting
2113. **B**	**2114. NIRVANA** (A) loss of auditory acuity; (B) nervous tension; (C) loss of courage; (D) muscular atrophy

33. A	**34. AMITY** (A) ill will; (B) hope; (C) pity; (D) friendship; (E) pleasure
143. A	**144. DENOUNCE** (A) abdicate; (B) accuse; (C) execute; (D) displace; (E) recite
253. C	**254. INANE** (A) energetic; (B) silly; (C) speechless; (D) unfit
363. D	**364. PRIVATION** (A) reward; (B) superiority in rank; (C) hardship; (D) suitability of behavior; (E) solitude
473. B	**474. UNEQUIVOCAL** (A) certain; (B) indefinite; (C) incorrect; (D) harmonious
583. C	**584. ATTENUATE** (A) command; (B) derive; (C) weaken; (D) strength
693. D	**694. CONGERIES** (A) intricate plots; (B) aggregation; (C) clique; (D) leave-takings
803. A	**804. EXEGESIS** (A) interpretation; (B) gradual exit; (C) model; (D) immunity
913. B	**914. IMPRIMATUR** (A) earliest stage; (B) sanction; (C) illumination; (D) printing shop
1023. C	**1024. NEBULOUS** (A) false; (B) basic; (C) cloudy; (D) starry

1133. C	**1134. PROSCENIUM** (A) amateur; (B) parade stand; (C) foreground; (D) first part of drama
1242. A	**1243. TENEBROUS** (A) gripping; (B) awaiting; (C) gloomy; (D) livable
1351. B	**1352. BLANDISH** (A) bleach; (B) flourish; (C) coax; (D) imprecate
1460. D	**1461. GECKO** (A) harness; (B) falcon; (C) lizard; (D) glove; (E) dwarf
1569. A	**1570. PALINDROME is illustrated by** (A) pal; (B) madam; (C) drum; (D) parchment re-used, with earlier writing erased
1678. A	**1679. SUTLER** (A) groom; (B) scullion; (C) house-boy; (D) army-follower; (E) gate-keeper
1787. C	**1788. ESTABLISH is to BEGIN as ABOLISH is to** (A) slavery; (B) wrong; (C) abolition; (D) end
1896. D	**1897. ARCHAEOLOGIST : ANTIQUITY : :** (A) theology : minister; (B) flower : horticulture; (C) ichthyologist : marine life; (D) Bible : psalms; (E) gold : silver
2005. D	**2006. PALLED** (A) exuberant; (B) shocked; (C) pierced; (D) weighted
2114. B	**2115. OBJURGATE** (A) appeal; (B) forswear; (C) praise; (D) importune

34. D	35. **AMPERSAND** (A) ammunition; (B) a type of currency; (C) an abbreviation; (D) a kind of illumination
144. B	145. **DEPLETE** (A) restrain; (B) corrupt; (C) despair; (D) exhaust; (E) spread out
254. B	255. **INCISIVE** (A) stimulating; (B) accidental; (C) brief; (D) penetrating; (E) final
364. C	365. **PROCRASTINATE** (A) tell a lie; (B) dismiss; (C) postpone; (D) furnish; (E) imitate
474. A	475. **UNSCRUPULOUS** (A) unprincipled; (B) unbalanced; (C) careless; (D) disfigured; (E) obstinate
584. C	585. **ATTRITION** (A) appeasement; (B) capitulation; (C) wearing away; (D) calming down
694. B	695. **CONSENSUS** (A) poll; (B) agreement; (C) conference; (D) attitude
804. A	805. **EXIGENT** (A) hasty; (B) discharged; (C) departing; (D) urgent
914. B	915. **IMPUGN** (A) repel; (B) cancel out; (C) impute; (D) attack
1024. C	1025. **NECROLOGY** (A) obituary notice; (B) disorder of nervous system; (C) black magic; (D) classified request

1134. C	**1135. PROSELYTE** (A) convert; (B) apostate; (C) agitator; (D) apostle
1243. C	**1244. TENUOUS** (A) tough; (B) uncertain; (C) thin; (D) nervous
1352. C	**1353. BODKIN** (A) guard; (B) ghoul; (C) raiment; (D) stiletto
1461. C	**1462. GIMCRACK** (A) bauble; (B) boring tool; (C) trick; (D) plumb
1570. B	**1571. PALINODE** (A) song of retraction; (B) fence post; (C) wedding hymn; (D) festival
1679. D	**1680. SVELTE** (A) wasteful; (B) slender; (C) suave; (D) indecisive
1788. D	**1789. DECEMBER is to JANUARY as LAST is to** (A) least; (B) worst; (C) month; (D) first
1897. C	**1898. SHOE : LEATHER : :** (A) passage : ship; (B) trail : wagon; (C) journey : boat; (D) highway : asphalt; (E) car : engine
2006. A	**2007. GAUD** (A) epithet; (B) simplicity; (C) spur; (D) taunt
2115. C	**2116. ONEIROMANCY** (A) interpretation of actual occurrences; (B) astrology; (C) fortune-telling by cards; (D) phrenology

35. C	**36. ANALOGOUS** (A) incongruous; (B) parallel; (C) viscous; (D) artificial
145. D	**146. DEPUTY** (A) arranger; (B) detective; (C) fugitive; (D) substitute; (E) cleanser
255. D	**256. INCLEMENT** (A) merciful; (B) sloping; (C) harsh; (D) disastrous; (E) personal
365. C	**366. PROCUREMENT** (A) acquisition; (B) resolution; (C) healing; (D) importance; (E) miracle
475. A	**476. USURP** (A) seize by force; (B) accompanying; (C) become useful; (D) move cityward; (E) return
585. C	**586. AUREOLE** (A) nesting place for birds; (B) rising light of morning; (C) distinctive atmosphere; (D) ring of encircling light
695. B	**696. CONTEMN** (A) scorn; (B) confine in prison; (C) sentence; (D) compete
805. D	**806. EXIGUOUS** (A) basically required; (B) sparse; (C) explanatory; (D) discriminating
915. D	**916. INAMORATA** (A) nameless person; (B) cognomen; (C) sweetheart; (D) lovelorn person
1025. A	**1026. NECROMANCY** (A) obituary notice; (B) magic; (C) fanciful medieval tale; (D) servility

1135. A	1136. **PROSODY** (A) science of verse forms; (B) dull style; (C) principles of prose style; (D) hymn of praise
1244. C	1245. **TERMAGANT** (A) white ant; (B) goal; (C) shrew; (D) permanent tenure
1353. D	1354. **BOLE** (A) seed pod; (B) round mass of medicine; (C) tree trunk; (D) goblet
1462. A	1463. **GIMLET** (A) adze; (B) small boring tool; (C) countersink; (D) auger
1571. A	1572. **PALLADIUM** (A) symbol of protection; (B) source of atomic power; (C) temple of the ancient gods; (D) medieval knight
1680. B	1681. **SYBARITE** (A) stoic; (B) parasite; (C) voluptuary; (D) ascetic
1789. D	1790. **GIANT is to DWARF as LARGE is to** (A) big; (B) monster; (C) queer; (D) small
1898. D	1899. **SERF : FEUDALISM : :** (A) laissez faire : tariff; (B) conservative : radical; (C) entrepreneur : capitalism; (D) child : parent; (E) farm : castle
2007. B	2008. **CAREEN** (A) hurtle; (B) whirl around; (C) stand upright; (D) move at break-neck speed
2116. A	2117. **OUTRÉ** (A) barren; (B) out-of-bounds; (C) usual; (D) stylish

36. **B**	**37. ANECDOTE** (A) equipment; (B) remedy for poison; (C) brief narrative; (D) inquiry; (E) hysteria
146. **D**	**147. DERELICT** (A) abandoned; (B) widowed; (C) faithful; (D) insincere; (E) hysterical
256. **C**	**257. INCOHERENT** (A) irritable; (B) uncomfortable; (C) disconnected; (D) unequaled; (E) ineffective
366. **A**	**367. PRODIGAL** (A) wasteful; (B) marvelous; (C) ominous; (D) harmless
476. **A**	**477. VACILLATE** (A) waver; (B) defeat; (C) favor; (D) endanger; (E) humiliate
586. **D**	**587. AUTOCLAVE** (A) steam apparatus; (B) despotic ruler; (C) airplane freight; (D) trustworthy assistant
696. **A**	**697. CONTIGUOUS** (A) extended; (B) broken; (C) opposed; (D) adjacent
806. **B**	**807. EXORCISE** (A) bring back to life; (B) make a pact with the devil; (C) wring the hands; (D) drive off an evil spirit
916. **C**	**917. INCIPIENT** (A) passive; (B) underhanded; (C) infected; (D) initial
1026. **B**	**1027. NEFARIOUS** (A) incomparable; (B) heinous; (C) ineffective; (D) opposing

1136. A	1137. **PROTOCOL** (A) Roman governor; (B) favorable legal opinion; (C) accomplice; (D) diplomatic etiquette
1245. C	1246. **TERMINOLOGY** (A) technical terms; (B) boundary; (C) fortification; (D) basis of agreement
1354. C	1355. **BOSCAGE** (A) Russian wolfhound; (B) thickets; (C) nutritious drink; (D) complete nonsense
1463. B	1464. **GLOZE** (A) doze; (B) extenuate; (C) glimpse; (D) realize
1572. A	1573. **PARACLETE** (A) dancer; (B) example; (C) contradiction; (D) advocate; (E) pattern
1681. C	1682. **SYNDIC** (A) audit; (B) investment; (C) corporation; (D) business agent
1790. D	1791. **ENGINE is to CABOOSE as BEGINNING is to** (A) commence; (B) cabin; (C) end; (D) train
1899. C	1900. **FIN : FISH : :** (A) engine : auto; (B) propeller : aeroplane; (C) five : ten; (D) teeth : stomach; (E) leg : chair
2008. C	2009. **DOLT** (A) prankster; (B) clever fellow; (C) manikin; (D) hobbledehoy
2117. C	2118. **PALINODE** (A) song of reassertion; (B) fence post; (C) wedding hymn; (D) festival

37. C	38. ANGUISH (A) awkwardness; (B) rage; (C) torment; (D) old age; (E) resentment
147. A	148. DERIDE (A) plead; (B) mock; (C) appeal; (D) surprise; (E) obligate
257. C	258. INCONSISTENT (A) insane; (B) senatorial; (C) undeviating; (D) contradictory; (E) faithful
367. A	368. PROFICIENCY (A) wisdom; (B) oversupply; (C) expertness; (D) advancement; (E) sincerity
477. A	478. VALANCE (A) chemical; (B) strength; (C) curtain; (D) esteem
587. A	588. AVARICE (A) profligacy; (B) cruelty; (C) greed; (D) insistence
697. D	698. CONTUMACIOUS (A) stubbornly disobedient; (B) deservedly disgraced; (C) unduly pompous; (D) gravely libelous
807. D	808. EXPATIATE (A) clear of guilt; (B) atone for; (C) emit the last breath; (D) enlarge on
917. D	918. INCOMMENSURABLE (A) requiring limitless care; (B) unbounded; (C) not condensable; (D) having no common measure
1027. B	1028. NEMESIS (A) nightmare; (B) one who bears the same title; (C) retributive justice; (D) climax of a story

1137. D	**1138. PRURIENT** (A) innocent; (B) putrescent; (C) lewd; (D) genuine; (E) atoning
1246. A	**1247. TESTILY** (A) irritably; (B) professionally; (C) proudly; (D) experimentally
1355. B	**1356. BOUTIQUE** (A) flower garden; (B) small retail store; (C) boxing arena; (D) merry-go-round
1464. B	**1465. GLYPTOGRAPHY** (A) exploring; (B) writing; (C) spying; (D) engraving
1573. D	**1574. PARADIGM** (A) model; (B) syllogism; (C) perfection; (D) similar case at law
1682. D	**1683. SYNDROME** (A) part of a motor; (B) group of symptoms; (C) buzzing noise; (D) type of virus
1791. C	**1792. DISMAL is to CHEERFUL as DARK is to** (A) sad; (B) stars; (C) night; (D) bright
1900. B	**1901. PULP : PAPER : :** (A) rope : hemp; (B) box : package; (C) paper : package; (D) yarn : fabric; (E) cellulose : rayon
2009. B	**2010. EBULLIENT** (A) capricious; (B) bizarre; (C) vapid; (D) destructive
2118. A	**2119. PELAGIC** (A) landlocked; (B) horny; (C) terrestrial; (D) furry

38. C	**39. ANIMATE** (A) paint; (B) praise highly; (C) enliven; (D) suggest indirectly; (E) debate
148. B	**149. DERISION** (A) disgust; (B) ridicule; (C) fear; (D) anger; (E) heredity
258. D	**259. INCREDIBLE** (A) threatening; (B) unbelievable; (C) incoherent; (D) irremediable
368. C	**369. PROFOUND** (A) deep; (B) disrespectful; (C) plentiful; (D) positive; (E) expert
478. C	**479. VEHEMENT** (A) thorough; (B) unexpected; (C) forceful; (D) smooth-running; (E) airy
588. C	**589. AVIDITY** (A) speed; (B) friendliness; (C) thirst; (D) greediness
698. A	**699. CONTUMACY** (A) adeptness; (B) slander; (C) defiance; (D) conceit
808. D	**809. EXPATRIATED** (A) demolished; (B) reinstated; (C) incarcerated; (D) banished
918. D	**919. INCUBUS** (A) nightmare; (B) egg hatched in incubator; (C) rain cloud; (D) geometric figure
1028. C	**1029. NEOPHYTE** (A) new species; (B) beginner; (C) marine plant; (D) visitor

1138. C	1139. PUERILE (A) barren; (B) pure; (C) foolish; (D) ignorant
1247. A	1248. THERAPEUTIC (A) contaminated; (B) infectious; (C) sterilized; (D) curative
1356. B	1357. BUCKLER (A) boss; (B) stress; (C) slash; (D) protection; (E) marriage
1465. D	1466. GNOME (A) sundial; (B) maxim; (C) mystery; (D) fawn; (E) reddish brown
1574. A	1575. PARTURITION (A) division of territory; (B) discrepancy in allotment; (C) childbirth; (D) dietary regimen
1683. B	1684. TABOR (A) drum; (B) guillotine; (C) table; (D) note; (E) prohibition
1792. D	1793. QUARREL is to ENEMY as AGREE is to (A) friend; (B) disagree; (C) agreeable; (D) foe
1901. E	1902. SKIN : MAN : : (A) scales: fur; (B) hide : hair; (C) walls : room; (D) roof : house; (E) clothes : lady
2010. C	2011. APOGEE (A) introductory remarks; (B) zenith; (C) figure of speech; (D) perigee
2119. C	2120. PETTIFOG (A) practice law in an honest way; (B) spread smoke and haze; (C) obstruct vision; (D) shrink cloth

39. C	**40. ANTITHESIS** (A) contrast; (B) balance; (C) parallel; (D) anxiety
149. B	**150. DESIGNATE** (A) draw; (B) expel; (C) permit; (D) name; (E) repeat
259. B	**260. INDIGNATION** (A) poverty; (B) anger; (C) exaggeration; (D) mercy; (E) publicity
369. A	**370. PROFUSION** (A) declaration; (B) abundance; (C) skillfulness; (D) depth; (E) anxiety
479. C	**480. VENEER** (A) respect; (B) arrival; (C) poison; (D) summons; (E) gloss
589. D	**590. AVUNCULAR** (A) pertaining to an uncle; (B) concerning a boil; (C) genealogical; (D) palliative
699. C	**700. CONTUMELY** (A) insolence; (B) noisiness; (C) design; (D) consideration
809. D	**810. EXPIATE** (A) enlarge; (B) atone; (C) erode; (D) decry
919. A	**920. INCULCATE** (A) deceive; (B) arouse; (C) incriminate; (D) instill
1029. B	**1030. NEPOTISM** (A) despotism; (B) favoritism; (C) nihilism; (D) stoicism

1139. C	**1140. PUNCTILIOUS** (A) accepted; (B) final; (C) prompt; (D) careful
1248. D	**1249. THESAURUS** (A) treasury; (B) ancient reptile; (C) creed; (D) Greek official
1357. D	**1358. BUTTE** (A) broad plain; (B) rifle range; (C) isolated hill; (D) large cask
1466. B	**1467. GODOWN** (A) descent; (B) warehouse; (C) incline; (D) sacrilege
1575. C	**1576. PASSIM** (A) inactive; (B) secretive; (C) everywhere; (D) perennial
1684. A	**1685. TANDEM** (A) one behind another; (B) in the meantime; (C) in full chase; (D) equivalent in value
1793. A	**1794. RAZOR is to SHARP as HOE is to** (A) bury; (B) dull; (C) cuts; (D) tree
1902. C	**1903. RAIN : DROP : :** (A) ice : winter; (B) cloud : sky; (C) flake : snow; (D) ocean : stream; (E) mankind : man
2011. D	**2012. DOUGHTY** (A) cowardly; (B) pasty; (C) invincible; (D) vacillating
2120. A	**2121. PLASHY** (A) tawdry; (B) rainy; (C) pretentious; (D) dry

40. **A**	**41. APERTURE** (A) basement; (B) opening; (C) phantom; (D) protective coloring; (E) light refreshment
150. **D**	**151. DESPONDENCY** (A) relief; (B) gratitude; (C) dejection; (D) hatred; (E) poverty
260. **B**	**261. INFAMOUS** (A) detestable; (B) humble; (C) gloomy; (D) scholarly; (E) unsuspected
370. **B**	**371. PROLIFIC** (A) fertile; (B) verbose; (C) ordinary; (D) sterile
480. **E**	**481. VERBATIM** (A) word for word; (B) at will; (C) without fail; (D) in secret; (E) in summary
590. **A**	**591. AWRY** (A) ungraceful; (B) distorted; (C) monstrous; (D) cautious
700. **A**	**701. CONTUMELIOUS** (A) mildly reproachful; (B) compromising; (C) disdainful; (D) genuinely contrite
810. **B**	**811. EXPONENTIAL** (A) discursive; (B) involving exponents; (C) neglecting explanations; (D) advocating
920. **D**	**921. INCURSION** (A) invective; (B) infusion; (C) invasion; (D) incision
1030. **B**	**1031. NETHER** (A) waterproof; (B) restrained; (C) lower; (D) nor yet

1140. D	**1141. PUNDIT** (A) prosy speaker; (B) witty saying; (C) learned man; (D) harsh judge
1249. A	**1250. THROE** (A) threshing machine; (B) violent pang; (C) turning point; (D) floating ice
1358. C	**1359. CABALA** (A) voodoo symbols; (B) medieval tribunal; (C) occult doctrine; (D) conspiratorial gathering
1467. B	**1468. GRAVAMEN** (A) grievance; (B) solemnity; (C) carved idol; (D) serving vessel
1576. C	**1577. PASTICHE** (A) imitative composition; (B) dessert; (C) forgotten event; (D) decoration
1685. A	**1686. TAMP** (A) pound down; (B) tread clumsily; (C) curl; (D) bind firmly
1794. B	**1795. WINTER is to SUMMER as COLD is to** (A) freeze; (B) warm; (C) wet; (D) January
1903. E	**1904. RAISIN : PRUNE : :** (A) apricot : currant; (B) grape : plum; (C) orange : grapefruit; (D) kumquat : orange; (E) citron : marmalade
2012. A	**2013. CONTEMN** (A) recognize; (B) confine; (C) sentence; (D) compete
2121. D	**2122. REPINE** (A) approve; (B) retract; (C) relax; (D) confess

41. **B**	**42. APPARITION** (A) skeleton; (B) fort; (C) ghost; (D) dream; (E) insect
151. **C**	**152. DETACHMENT** (A) liking; (B) chance; (C) activity; (D) secrecy; (E) aloofness
261. **A**	**262. INFER** (A) surprise; (B) hope; (C) disagree; (D) conclude; (E) shift quickly
371. **A**	**372. PROPENSITY** (A) inclination; (B) propriety; (C) appearance; (D) plot
481. **A**	**482. VERBOSITY** (A) stubbornness; (B) action; (C) wordiness; (D) speed
591. **B**	**592. BAGATELLE** (A) suitcase; (B) trifle; (C) riddle; (D) sea shell
701. **C**	**702. CONVIVIAL** (A) carefree; (B) occupying jointly; (C) contemporaneous; (D) gay
811. **B**	**812. EX POST FACTO** (A) retrospective; (B) prior; (C) posthumous; (D) causative
921. **C**	**922. INDIGENOUS** (A) confused; (B) undignified; (C) poverty-stricken; (D) inherent
1031. **C**	**1032. NIGGARDLY** (A) dark; (B) critical; (C) mean; (D) intensive

1141. C	**1142. PURLIEU** (A) outlying region; (B) range of activity; (C) kerchief worn about the neck; (D) small waterfall
1250. B	**1251. THROW A SOP TO CERBERUS** (A) salve one's conscience; (B) divide into unequal shares; (C) pay piper for calling tune; (D) give a bribe in order to quiet a troublesome person
1359. C	**1360. CACHINNATION** (A) conspiracy to rob; (B) immoderate laughter; (C) noisy riot; (D) subterranean vibration
1468. A	**1469. GRAVID** (A) harsh; (B) pregnant; (C) unyielding; (D) serious
1577. A	**1578. PATINA** (A) local dialect; (B) base metal; (C) Italian folk-dance; (D) chemical coating
1686. A	**1687. TARE** (A) tax on salt; (B) deduction from gross weight to allow for container; (C) deity; (D) rip
1795. B	**1796. RUDDER is to SHIP as TAIL is to** (A) sail; (B) bird; (C) dog; (D) cat
1904. B	**1905. CONSTELLATION : STARS : :** (A) continent : peninsula; (B) state : country; (C) archipelago : island; (D) dollar : penny; (E) library : book
2013. A	**2014. PECULATOR** (A) gambler; (B) herdsman; (C) benefactor; (D) finder
2122. A	**2123. RAFFISH** (A) dour; (B) carefree; (C) sporty; (D) reputable

42. C	**43. APPREHENSIVE** (A) quiet; (B) firm; (C) curious; (D) sincere; (E) fearful
152. E	**153. DETERRENT** (A) restraining; (B) cleansing; (C) deciding; (D) concluding; (E) crumbling
262. D	**263. INFERNAL** (A) immodest; (B) incomplete; (C) domestic; (D) second-rate; (E) fiendish
372. A	**373. PROSELYTE** (A) convert; (B) prosecute; (C) presage; (D) acolyte
482. C	**483. VERSATILE** (A) imaginative; (B) many-sided; (C) proud; (D) upright; (E) self-centered
592. B	**593. BAILIWICK** (A) fabled creature; (B) small burial chapel; (C) degree of security; (D) district of a bailiff
702. D	**703. CONVOLUTED** (A) knotted; (B) transformed; (C) accompanied; (D) coiled
812. A	**813. EXTENUATE** (A) excuse; (B) project; (C) stretch; (D) blame
922. D	**923. INDURATE** (A) harden; (B) prolong; (C) endow; (D) suffer
1032. C	**1033. NOISOME** (A) ear-splitting; (B) uproarious; (C) noxious; (D) teasing

1142. A	**1143. PURLOIN** (A) cleanse; (B) steal; (C) stain; (D) knit
1251. D	**1252. TIRADE** (A) plan of strategy; (B) harsh speech; (C) procession; (D) coronet
1360. B	**1361. CACOGRAPHY** (A) cryptogram; (B) poor spelling; (C) good writing; (D) earth science
1469. B	**1470. GROAT** (A) silver coin; (B) small animal; (C) edible fish; (D) worthless trifle
1578. D	**1579. PEDUNCLE** (A) flower stalk; (B) pawnbroker; (C) gabled roof; (D) pediculate fish
1687. B	**1688. TERTIAN** (A) recurring; (B) subordinate; (C) intermediate; (D) remote in time
1796. B	**1797. GRANARY is to WHEAT as LIBRARY is to** (A) desk; (B) books; (C) paper; (D) librarian
1905. C	**1906. BOOKKEEPING : ACCOUNTANCY : :** (A) reporter : editor; (B) typist : stenography; (C) lawyer : judge; (D) boy : man; (E) student : teacher
2014. C	**2015. ENCLAVE** (A) territory which is part of common group; (B) settlement surrounded by palisades; (C) papal summons to a consistory; (D) prison yard
2123. D	**2124. PROVENANCE** (A) last resting place; (B) foresight; (C) scion's inheritance; (D) provisions

43. E	44. ARBITER (A) friend; (B) judge; (C) drug; (D) tree surgeon; (E) truant
153. A	154. DETRIMENTAL (A) abhorrent; (B) determined; (C) injurious; (D) intelligent
263. E	264. INFILTRATE (A) pass through; (B) stop; (C) consider; (D) challenge openly; (E) meet secretly
373. A	374. PROTAGONIST (A) prophet; (B) explorer; (C) talented child; (D) convert; (E) leading character
483. B	484. VESTIGE (A) design; (B) strap; (C) trace; (D) bar
593. D	594. BAIZE (A) cereal plant; (B) medicinal plant; (C) tree marking; (D) soft fabric
703. D	704. CORUSCATE (A) indent; (B) tear; (C) oxidize; (D) sparkle
813. A	814. EXTRINSIC (A) germane; (B) eccentric; (C) uncultivated; (D) external
923. A	924. INEFFABLE (A) ineffective; (B) irretrievable; (C) unpleasant; (D) unspeakable
1033. C	1034. NUANCE (A) delicate shading; (B) prejudice; (C) birthmark; (D) disturbance

1143. B	1144. PURPORT (A) design; (B) account; (C) meaning; (D) result
1252. B	1253. TORPID (A) firing rapidly; (B) vivacious; (C) swift; (D) dormant
1361. B	1362. CADGE (A) beguile; (B) nag; (C) steal; (D) beg
1470. A	1471. GUERDON (A) obstacle; (B) emblazoned shield; (C) reward; (D) motto
1579. A	1580. PEIGNOIR (A) dressing gown; (B) knot formed by twisting and pinning up long hair; (C) inclination or desire; (D) fur collar
1688. A	1689. TESSELLATE (A) quiver uncontrollably; (B) arrange in a checkered pattern; (C) adorn with random scraps of material; (D) dry up rapidly
1797. B	1798. INTELLIGENCE is to UNDERSTANDING as STUPIDITY is to (A) ignorance; (B) pleasure; (C) school; (D) unhappiness
1906. A	1907. RUBBER : FLEXIBILITY : : (A) iron : pliability; (B) iron : elasticity; (C) steel : rigidity; (D) synthetics : natural; (E) wood : plastic
2015. A	2016. IRENIC (A) easily pleased; (B) sarcastic; (C) warlike; (D) non-ferrous
2124. A	2125. SACERDOTAL (A) priestly; (B) baggy; (C) sugary; (D) profane

44. **B**	**45. ARDENT** (A) eager; (B) silvery; (C) difficult; (D) youthful; (E) argumentative
154. **C**	**155. DEVASTATION** (A) desolation; (B) displeasure; (C) dishonor; (D) neglect; (E) religious fervor
264. **A**	**265. INGENUE is a term used in referring to** (A) the fashion; (B) a state; (C) a medicine; (D) the stage
374. **E**	**375. PROWESS** (A) fear; (B) cane; (C) roving; (D) valor
484. **C**	**485. VETERINARY** (A) retired soldier; (B) civil servant; (C) hospital; (D) animal doctor
594. **D**	**595. BANAL** (A) forbidden; (B) sad; (C) poisonous; (D) commonplace
704. **D**	**705. CORVETTE** (A) sea gull; (B) small cannon; (C) gunboat; (D) lace collar
814. **D**	**815. EXTIRPATE** (A) prevent; (B) extricate; (C) exaggerate; (D) eradicate
924. **D**	**925. INELUCTABLE** (A) unavoidable; (B) inscrutable; (C) approachable; (D) esoteric
1034. **A**	**1035. NUBILE** (A) obscure; (B) voluptuous; (C) marriageable; (D) oriental

1144. C	**1145. PUSILLANIMOUS** (A) stealthy; (B) timid; (C) weak; (D) wary
1253. D	**1254. TORTUOUS** (A) painful; (B) devious; (C) grim; (D) infectious
1362. D	**1363. A CADMEAN VICTORY is one in which** (A) the victory is won speedily; (B) the victor suffers as much as the vanquished; (C) the victor used his teeth; (D) air power gave the victor superiority
1471. C	**1472. GULES** (A) red; (B) green; (C) blue; (D) yellow
1580. A	**1581. PEJORATIVE** (A) privileged; (B) false; (C) hysterical; (D) depreciatory
1689. B	**1690. THANE** (A) slave; (B) lace; (C) landholder; (D) destitute; (E) skate
1798. A	**1799. SAND is to GLASS as CLAY is to** (A) stone; (B) hay; (C) bricks; (D) dirt
1907. C	**1908. ABSENCE : PRESENCE : :** (A) steady : secure; (B) safe : influential; (C) poor : influential; (D) fresh : canned; (E) stable : changeable
2016. C	**2017. MOUNTEBANK** (A) one who lives in a valley; (B) an honest person; (C) sea gull; (D) beggar
2125. D	**2126. UXORIOUS** (A) clamorous; (B) lavish in display; (C) loathing one's wife; (D) loving one's spouse

45. **A**	**46. ARID** (A) mountainous; (B) fragrant; (C) soiled; (D) dry; (E) productive
155. **A**	**156. DEVIATE** (A) destroy; (B) amplify; (C) dedicate; (D) wander
265. **D**	**266. INJUNCTION** (A) error; (B) attack; (C) injustice; (D) suggestion; (E) order
375. **D**	**376. PRUDENT** (A) critical; (B) cautious; (C) bluish; (D) unfinished; (E) outrageous
485. **D**	**486. VIGILANT** (A) forceful; (B) immoral; (C) alert; (D) sightless; (E) many-sided
595. **D**	**596. BANE** (A) blessing; (B) curse; (C) favor; (D) destiny
705. **C**	**706. COVERT** (A) envious; (B) secret; (C) timid; (D) protected
815. **D**	**816. FACETIOUS** (A) discontented; (B) imaginary; (C) jocular; (D) trivial
925. **A**	**926. INFESTED** (A) diseased; (B) surrounded; (C) overrun; (D) corrupted
1035. **C**	**1036. NUGATORY** (A) debatable; (B) chewy; (C) changeable; (D) worthless

1145. **B**	**1146. PUTATIVE** (A) powerful; (B) rotting; (C) supposed; (D) scolding
1254. **B**	**1255. TOUCHSTONE** (A) instrument for sharpening tools; (B) material for cleaning decks of ships; (C) test for worth; (D) fundamental cause
1363. **B**	**1364. CAIRN** (A) small boy; (B) base wretch; (C) cave; (D) memorial
1472. **A**	**1473. GULL** (A) foil; (B) zany; (C) henchman; (D) dupe; (E) hind
1581. **D**	**1532. PELAGIC** (A) horny; (B) landlocked; (C) oceanic; (D) furry
1690. **C**	**1691. THEWS** (A) attitude; (B) physical strength; (C) cuttings; (D) tree limbs
1799. **C**	**1800. DISLOYAL is to FAITHLESS as** **IMPERFECTION is to** (A) contamination; (B) depression; (C) foible; (D) decrepitude
1908. **E**	**1909. SAFETY VALVE : BOILER : :** (A) fuse : motor; (B) house : wire; (C) city : factory; (D) brake : automobile; (E) extinguisher : fire
2017. **B**	**2018. INCREDULOUS** (A) argumentative; (B) imaginative; (C) indifferent; (D) irreligious; (E) believing
2126. **C**	**2127. VELLEITY** (A) excusable error; (B) sentimental weeping; (C) strong wish; (D) unfulfilled longing

46. **D**	**47. ARROGANCE** (A) firmness; (B) greatness; (C) haughtiness; (D) surprise; (E) helpfulness
156. **D**	**157. DEVOID** (A) empty; (B) illegal; (C) affectionate; (D) pious; (E) annoying
266. **E**	**267. INSINUATE** (A) destroy; (B) hint; (C) do wrong; (D) accuse; (E) release
376. **B**	**377. PSEUDONYM** (A) title of nobility; (B) lack of a name; (C) family name; (D) pen name; (E) dishonorable name
486. **C**	**487. VINDICATE** (A) outrage; (B) waver; (C) enliven; (D) justify; (E) fuse
596. **B**	**597. BARMECIDE FEAST** (A) Lucullan repast; (B) murder at the dinner table; (C) false appearance of plenty; (D) hearty meal eaten by a condemned man
706. **B**	**707. COZEN** (A) cheat; (B) fondle; (C) tease; (D) persuade
816. **C**	**817. FACTIOUS** (A) artificial; (B) contentious; (C) compromising; (D) handmade
926. **C**	**927. INGENUOUS** (A) quick; (B) devious; (C) talented; (D) frank
036. **D**	**1037. NUMISMATICS** (A) science of coins; (B) study of postage stamps; (C) study of moths; (D) art of foretelling

1146. C	**1147. PYRRHIC VICTORY** (A) victory gained at too great a cost; (B) victory as a result of encirclement; (C) total destruction of the enemy; (D) victory as a result of a complete surprise
1255. C	**1256. TOUR DE FORCE** (A) ingenious accomplishment; (B) tower of strength; (C) stroke of policy; (D) change of direction
1364. D	**1365. CAJOLERY** (A) superstition; (B) wheedling; (C) obstreperousness; (D) drollery
1473. D	**1474. HABILE** (A) skillful; (B) weak; (C) needy; (D) untidy
1582. C	**1583. PELF** (A) thigh; (B) culvert; (C) imp; (D) booty
1691. B	**1692. THORP** (A) village; (B) lariat; (C) bolero; (D) incandescence
1800. C	**1801. TEARS is to SORROW as LAUGHTER is to** (A) joy; (B) smile; (C) girls; (D) grain
1909. A	**1910. SCHOLARLY : UNSCHOLARLY : :** (A) learned : ignorant; (B) wise : skilled; (C) scholarly : literary; (D) knowledge : books; (E) lies : knowledge
2018. E	**2019. PLACATE** (A) amuse; (B) antagonize; (C) embroil; (D) pity; (E) reject
2127. C	**2128. WHILOM** (A) intermittent; (B) old-fashioned; (C) future; (D) quaint

47. C	**48. ASPIRE** (A) fade away; (B) excite; (C) desire earnestly; (D) breathe heavily; (E) roughen
157. A	**158. DEXTERITY** (A) conceit; (B) skill; (C) insistence; (D) embarrassment; (E) guidance
267. B	**268. INSIPID** (A) disrespectful; (B) uninteresting; (C) persistent; (D) whole; (E) stimulating
377. D	**378. PUGNACIOUS** (A) sticky; (B) cowardly; (C) precise; (D) vigorous; (E) quarrelsome
487. D	**488. VIRULENT** (A) malignant; (B) luscious; (C) scolding; (D) manly
597. C	**598. BAROQUE** (A) Gallic; (B) grotesque; (C) Oriental; (D) angular
707. A	**708. CRASS** (A) ostentatious; (B) avaricious; (C) alluringly deceitful; (D) coarse
817. B	**818. FACTITIOUS** (A) accurate; (B) treacherous; (C) sham; (D) argumentative
927. D	**928. INGRATE** (A) ungrateful person; (B) traitor; (C) impostor; (D) culinary utensil
1037. A	**1038. OBDURATE** (A) stubborn; (B) long-lasting; (C) stupid; (D) apparent

1147. A	1148. QUERULOUS (A) furtive; (B) curious; (C) quavering; (D) complaining
1256. A	1257. TRACTABLE (A) docile; (B) exacting; (C) discernible; (D) strong
1365. B	1366. CALCARIFORM (A) stone-like; (B) spur-shaped; (C) cave-forming; (D) chalk-like
1474. A	1475. HALIDOM (A) martyrdom; (B) fief; (C) ancestry; (D) sanctuary
1583. D	1584. PEREGRINE (A) ambulatory; (B) deceptive; (C) odious; (D) alien
1692. A	1693. THRALL (A) soldier; (B) slave; (C) hero; (D) dwarf
1801. A	1802. COLD is to ICE as HEAT is to (A) lightning; (B) warm; (C) steam; (D) coat
1910. A	1911. IMMIGRATION : IMMIGRANT : : (A) file : knife; (B) travel : alien; (C) native : foreigner; (D) emigration : traveler; (E) nest : bird
2019. B	2020. COGNIZANT (A) afraid; (B) ignorant; (C) capable; (D) aware; (E) optimistic
2128. C Page 96	2129. SENTENCE COMPLETIONS *Directions:* Select from the lettered words or sets of words, the word or words which best complete the meaning of the statement as a whole.

48. **C**	**49. ASSERTION** (A) declaration; (B) abandonment; (C) agreement; (D) decoding; (E) appraisal
158. **B**	**159. DEXTEROUS** (A) divided; (B) harsh; (C) individual; (D) skillful; (E) evil
268. **B**	**269. INSTIGATE** (A) uphold; (B) conceal; (C) accuse; (D) renew; (E) provoke
378. **E**	**379. PUNGENT** (A) biting; (B) smooth; (C) quarrelsome; (D) wrong; (E) proud
488. **A**	**489. VISCOUS** (A) intestinal; (B) sticky; (C) glossy; (D) noxious
598. **B**	**599. BAROUCHE** (A) conveyance; (B) headgear; (C) vestment; (D) thicket
708. **D**	**709. CREPITATE** (A) enfeeble; (B) worsen; (C) depreciate; (D) crackle
818. **C**	**819. FALLOW** (A) idle land; (B) ensue; (C) inaccurate statement; (D) sickness
928. **A**	**929. INIMICAL** (A) incomparable; (B) unfriendly; (C) prohibitive; (D) without glory
1038. **A**	**1039. OBEISANCE** (A) attention; (B) bauble; (C) homage; (D) overweight

1148. D	**1149. QUIDNUNC** (A) subtle distinction; (B) sightseeing bus; (C) afternoon prayer; (D) busybody
1257. A	**1258. TRADUCE** (A) override; (B) tempt; (C) vilify; (D) barter
1366. B	**1367. CALENDER** (A) to press between rollers; (B) to tell time; (C) to make a chronology; (D) to standardize
1475. D	**1476. HALYARD** (A) sail; (B) spar; (C) flag; (D) rope
1584. D	**1585. PERQUISITE** (A) need; (B) daintiness; (C) incidental wages; (D) guile
1693. B	**1694. THRASONICAL** (A) brutal; (B) boastful; (C) idle; (D) royal
1802. C	**1803. REMUNERATIVE is to PROFITABLE as FRAUDULENT is to** (A) spying; (B) slander; (C) fallacious; (D) plausible; (E) reward
1911. B	**1912. GOVERNOR : STATE : :** (A) lieutenant : army; (B) ship : captain; (C) admiral : navy; (D) inmate : institution; (E) mother : home
2020. B	**2021. DISSONANCE** (A) disapproval; (B) disaster; (C) harmony; (D) disparity; (E) dissimilarity
Page 98	**2130. The ————— prowess of the pugilist ————— fear into his opponent.** (A) redoubtable - instilled; (B) supernatural - propelled; (C) probing - prevented; (D) pert - led

49. A	**50. ASSIDUOUS** (A) apart; (B) bilateral; (C) diligent; (D) sour
159. D	**160. DILATORY** (A) expanding; (B) delaying; (C) watery; (D) pickling
269. E	**270. INSUPERABLE** (A) incomprehensible; (B) elaborate; (C) unusual; (D) indigestible; (E) unconquerable
379. A	**380. PURGE** (A) knit; (B) chase; (C) pucker; (D) elope; (E) cleanse
489. B	**490. VIVACIOUS** (A) wild; (B) erratic; (C) disloyal; (D) lively; (E) direct
599. A	**600. BATHOS** (A) bitter satire; (B) deepest part of the sea; (C) sublime state; (D) strained pathetic effect
709. D	**710. CREPUSCULAR** (A) like crinkled fabric; (B) resembling twilight; (C) diminutive; (D) transitory
819. A	**820. FARRIER** (A) ship's carpenter; (B) litter of pigs; (C) blacksmith; (D) trainman
929. B	**930. INIQUITY** (A) persecution; (B) wickedness; (C) disparity; (D) irregularity
1039. C	**1040. OBFUSCATE** (A) block; (B) make unnecessary; (C) bewilder; (D) penetrate

1149. **D**	**1150. QUIESCENCE** (A) pentagon; (B) extract; (C) silence; (D) query
1258. **C**	**1259. TRAMMEL** (A) bore holes in; (B) stamp on; (C) impede; (D) blend into one mass
1367. **A**	**1368. CALUMET** (A) purge; (B) false accusation; (C) peace pipe; (D) dagger
1476. **D**	**1477. HANAPER** (A) hindrance; (B) plume; (C) gift; (D) uproar; (E) receptacle
1585. **C**	**1586. PERUKE** (A) jacket; (B) wig; (C) pipe; (D) illness
1694. **B**	**1695. TINE** (A) rare spice; (B) pointed prong; (C) infinitesimal amount; (D) electrical current
1803. **C**	**1804. AX is to WOODSMAN as AWL is to** (A) cut; (B) hew; (C) plumber; (D) pierce; (E) cobbler
1912. **C**	**1913. LETTER CARRIER : MAIL : :** (A) messenger : value; (B) delivery : easy; (C) government : fast; (D) courier : dispatch; (E) message : messenger
2021. **C**	**2022. TORSION** (A) bending; (B) compressing; (C) sliding; (D) stretching; (E) straightening
2130. **A** *Page* 100	**2131. His ————— nature will aid him in attaining** **success in this difficult job.** (A) imitative; (B) lackadaisical; (C) persevering; (D) rotund

| 50. | 51. ASEPTIC |
| C | (A) antique; (B) artistic; (C) sterile; (D) austere |

| 160. | 161. DIMINUTIVE |
| B | (A) proud; (B) slow; (C) small; (D) watery; (E) puzzling |

| 270. | 271. INTEGRITY |
| E | (A) honesty; (B) interest; (C) comfort; (D) width; (E) pride |

| 380. | 381. PUTREFY |
| E | (A) decay; (B) purify; (C) diminish; (D) penalize |

| 490. | 491. VOCIFEROUS |
| D | (A) energetic; (B) clamorous; (C) musical; (D) calmly |

| 600. | 601. BEATIFIC |
| D | (A) calm; (B) hesitant; (C) blissful; (D) throbbing |

| 710. | 711. "CROSS THE RUBICON" |
| B | (A) pass into oblivion; (B) overcome almost insurmountable difficulties; (C) take an irrevocable step; (D) change one's identity |

| 820. | 821. FATUITY |
| C | (A) foolishness; (B) smugness; (C) casualty; (D) obesity |

| 930. | 931. INNOCUOUS |
| B | (A) guiltless; (B) noxious; (C) harmless; (D) immune |

| 1040. | 1041. OBITER DICTUM |
| C | (A) incidental remark; (B) prayer for the dead; (C) reputation; (D) rumor |

1150. C	1151. QUIXOTIC (A) amalgamated; (B) impracticable; (C) idealistic; (D) incessant
1259. C	1260. TRAUMA (A) vibration; (B) deafness; (C) shock; (D) revelation
1368. C	1369. CANNEL (A) conduit; (B) perfume; (C) coal; (D) nut
1477. E	1478. HARRIDAN (A) hound; (B) tormentor; (C) bigot; (D) vixen
1586. B	1587. PETARD (A) hook; (B) crane; (C) ram; (D) bomb
1695. B	1696. TRANSMOGRIFIED (A) transported in ecstasy; (B) changed as by magic; (C) disinterred; (D) felled by terror
1804. E	1805. SURGEON is to SCALPEL as BUTCHER is to (A) mallet; (B) cleaver; (C) chisel; (D) wrench; (E) medicine
1913. D	1914. CLOTH : COAT : : (A) doll : cover; (B) gingham : dress; (C) dressmaker : suit; (D) cover : box; (E) yarn : wool
2022. E	2023. ACCRUED (A) subtracted; (B) incidental; (C) miscellaneous; (D) special; (E) unearned
2131. C	2132. Since he is a teacher of English, we would not expect him to be guilty of a ————. (A) solecism; (B) schism; (C) stanchion; (D) freshet

51. **C**	**52. ASSIMILATE** (A) absorb; (B) imitate; (C) maintain; (D) outrun; (E) curb
161. **C**	**162. DIRE** (A) grimy; (B) noisy; (C) stubborn; (D) dreadful; (E) sharp-edged
271. **A**	**272. INTERLOPER** (A) alien; (B) intruder; (C) questioner; (D) magician; (E) rainmaker
381. **A**	**382. QUAGMIRE** (A) bog; (B) goal; (C) monogram; (D) quarrel
491. **B**	**492. VOGUE** (A) picture; (B) history; (C) cloudiness; (D) popularity; (E) mischief
601. **C**	**602. BEATITUDE** (A) vision; (B) defeat; (C) blessedness; (D) gratitude
711. **C**	**712. CRUCIAL** (A) decisive; (B) difficult; (C) irritable; (D) painful
821. **A**	**822. FATUOUS** (A) pompous; (B) inane; (C) fleshy; (D) inexact
931. **C**	**932. INSOUCIANT** (A) substitute; (B) carefree; (C) irreconcilable; (D) tasteless
1041. **A**	**1042. OBLATION** (A) coercive measure; (B) religious offering; (C) responsibility; (D) forgetfulness

1151. **B**	**1152. QUOD VIDE** (A) quarterly volume; (B) question answered; (C) which see; (D) which was to be demonstrated
1260. **C**	**1261. TRAVESTY** (A) long journey; (B) installation ceremony; (C) burlesque; (D) simple task
1369. **C**	**1370. CANOROUS** (A) hungry; (B) melodious; (C) cacophonous; (D) hound-like
1478. **D**	**1479. HIGGLE** (A) beguile; (B) bedim; (C) chaffer; (D) exorcise
1587. **D**	**1588. PETROGLYPH** (A) silicon; (B) mermaid; (C) rock carving; (D) mysterious manifestation
1696. **B**	**1697. TRENCHERMAN** (A) hearty eater; (B) construction worker; (C) day laborer; (D) servile follower
1805. **B**	**1806. CAT is to FELINE as HORSE is to** (A) equine; (B) tiger; (C) quadruped; (D) carnivorous; (E) vulpine
1914. **B**	**1915. BOAT : DOCK : :** (A) wing : strut; (B) engine : chassis; (C) contents : box; (D) verb : sentence; (E) dirigible : hangar
2023. **A**	**2024. EFFRONTERY** (A) bad taste; (B) conceit; (C) dishonesty; (D) shyness; (E) snobbishness
2132. **A** *Page* 104	**2133. The servant's attitude was so –––––, it would have been ––––– to a sincere person.** (A) natal - clear; (B) hybrid - available; (C) syco- phantic - obnoxious; (D) doleful - responsible

52. A	**53. ATOMIC** (A) combustible; (B) minute; (C) crystalline; (D) ambient
162. D	**163. DISCRIMINATE** (A) fail; (B) delay; (C) accuse; (D) distinguish; (E) reject
272. B	**273. INTERMINABLE** (A) periodic; (B) unbearable; (C) well-blended; (D) short-lived; (E) unending
382. A	**383. QUIRK** (A) opportunity; (B) questioning; (C) peculiarity; (D) mistaken identity; (E) persistent annoyance
492. D	**493. VOLITION** (A) electrical power; (B) brute strength; (C) quantity; (D) will; (E) large print
602. C	**603. BEGUILE** (A) irk; (B) mislead; (C) befriend; (D) waste
712. A	**713. CRUET** (A) fork; (B) oar; (C) bottle; (D) game
822. B	**823. FEBRILE** (A) fraying; (B) mitigating; (C) efficacious; (D) feverish
932. B	**933. INSOUCIANCE** (A) insolence; (B) indifference; (C) animation; (D) disrespect
1042. B	**1043. OBLOQUY** (A) sacrifice; (B) forgetfulness; (C) calumny; (D) indirectness

1152. C	1153. RAFFISH (A) prurient; (B) disreputable; (C) splenetic; (D) lackadaisical
1261. C	1262. TRICE (A) small circular saw; (B) very short time; (C) insignificant matter; (D) metal framework
1370. B	1371. CANT (A) song; (B) ode; (C) gait; (D) jargon
1479. C	1480. HYMENEAL (A) religious song; (B) marriage song; (C) blunt instrument; (D) sharp instrument
1588. C	1589. PETTIFOG (A) practice law in a tricky way; (B) spread smoke and haze; (C) obstruct vision; (D) shrink cloth
1697. A	1698. TRIVET (A) document conferring a military rank; (B) small vial for vinegar, oil, etc.; (C) support for hot vessels; (D) evergreen shrub
1806. A	1807. ADVERSITY is to HAPPINESS as VEHEMENCE is to (A) misfortune; (B) gayety; (C) troublesome; (D) petulance; (E) serenity
1915. E	1916. OAT : BUSHEL : : (A) wheat : grain; (B) hardness : usefulness; (C) gold : karat; (D) diamond : carat; (E) ornament : case
2024. D	2025. ACQUIESCENCE (A) advice; (B) advocacy; (C) opposition; (D) friendliness; (E) compliance
2133. C	2134. One would expect a serf to ————— to a lord. (A) arrogate; (B) apprize; (C) circumscribe; (D) truckle

53. B	**54. ATONE** (A) praise; (B) evaluate; (C) make amends; (D) sing softly; (E) rest
163. D	**164. DISDAINFUL** (A) scornful; (B) disgraceful; (C) willful; (D) ungrateful; (E) unhealthful
273. E	**274. INTERMITTENT** (A) periodic; (B) deep-seated; (C) mixed; (D) countless; (E) brief
383. C	**384. RATIONALIZE** (A) rattle; (B) explain by reason; (C) limit consumption; (D) charge
493. D	**494. VOLUBLE** (A) bulky; (B) glib; (C) desirable; (D) malleable
603. B	**604. BEHEMOTH** (A) large animal; (B) flying insect; (C) poisonous flower; (D) rare mineral
713. C	**714. CUL-DE-SAC** (A) discharge; (B) dry sherry; (C) collection; (D) blind alley
823. D	**824. FECKLESS** (A) worthless; (B) unmannerly; (C) dauntless; (D) foul
933. B	**934. INSIDIOUS** (A) treacherous; (B) lacking finesse; (C) unilateral; (D) meaningless
1043. C	**1044. OBSECRATE** (A) curse; (B) secrete; (C) send; (D) entreat

1153. B	**1154. RAMIFY** (A) butt; (B) branch; (C) force; (D) strengthen
1262. B	**1263. TRUCKLE** (A) transport; (B) submit obsequiously; (C) tighten securely; (D) barter
1371. D	**1372. CARAPACE** (A) shell covering all or part of an animal; (B) gargoyle; (C) playful leap or skip; (D) panoply
1480. B	**1481. HYPERACUSIA** (A) abnormal hearing; (B) accusation; (C) figure of speech; (D) exaggeration
1589. A	**1590. PHAETON** (A) nemesis; (B) light carriage; (C) prophet; (D) side-car
1698. C	**1699. TROGLODYTE** (A) tropical bird; (B) cave dweller; (C) misogynist; (D) dwarf
1807. E	**1808. NECKLACE is to ADORNMENT as MEDAL is to** (A) jewel; (B) metal; (C) bravery; (D) bronze; (E) decoration
1916. D	**1917. PHYSIOLOGY : SCIENCE : :** (A) pyschology : psychiatry; (B) law : profession; (C) contract : suit; (D) painting : art; (E) worker : work
2025. C	**2026. RETICENT** (A) fidgety; (B) repetitious; (C) talkative; (D) restful; (E) truthful
2134. D *Page* 108	**2135. Any public officer who allows bribery to flourish should be subject to ————.** (A) stringency; (B) vagary; (C) stricture; (D) apologue

54. **C**	**55. ATROCIOUS** (A) brutal; (B) innocent; (C) shrunken; (D) yellowish; (E) unsound
164. **A**	**165. DISPARAGE** (A) separate; (B) compare; (C) refuse; (D) belittle; (E) imitate
274. **A**	**275. INTERVENE** (A) induce; (B) insert; (C) interfere; (D) solve
384. **B**	**385. RAVAGE** (A) lay waste; (B) complain; (C) talk wildly; (D) rush about; (E) admire
494. **B**	**495. VULNERABLE** (A) usually harmless; (B) slyly greedy; (C) poisonous; (D) deeply religious; (E) open to attack
604. **A**	**605. BELLICOSE** (A) indignant; (B) resonant; (C) warlike; (D) beauteous
714. **D**	**715. CULT** (A) club; (B) mob; (C) party; (D) sect
824. **A**	**825. FECUND** (A) fruitful; (B) decaying; (C) offensive; (D) feverish
934. **A**	**935. INSUFFERABLE** (A) rebellious; (B) invincible; (C) intolerable; (D) without pain
D44. **D**	**1045. OBSOLESCENCE** (A) old age; (B) renunciation; (C) disuse; (D) indecency

1154. **B**	**1155. RANCOR** (A) ill will; (B) acidity; (C) unpleasant odor; (D) heart ailment
1263. **B**	**1264. TRUCULENCE** (A) involvement; (B) heaviness; (C) peacefulness; (D) cruelty
1372. **A**	**1373. CAROMED** (A) rebounded; (B) duly licensed; (C) abutted; (D) reversed
1481. **A**	**1482. HYPERTROPHIED** (A) enlarged; (B) diseased; (C) wasted; (D) useless
1590. **B**	**1591. PHARISAICAL** (A) charitable; (B) reconcilable; (C) intransigent; (D) hypocritical
1699. **B**	**1700. TROPE** (A) heliograph; (B) marigold; (C) figure of speech; (D) pertaining to nutrition
1808. **E**	**1809. GUN is to HOLSTER as SWORD is to** (A) pistol; (B) scabbard; (C) warrior; (D) slay; (E) plunder
1917. **D**	**1918. INSTINCT : EXPERIENCE : :** (A) imagination : reality; (B) thought : idea; (C) sight : image; (D) development : project; (E) research : development
2026. **C**	**2027. PSEUDO** (A) deep; (B) obvious; (C) honest; (D) provoking; (E) spiritual
2135. **C** *Page* 110	**2136. The old man was so ————— that he refused to buy food.** (A) parsimonious; (B) prescient; (C) prolix; (D) affluent

55. **A**	**56. ATTRIBUTE** (A) characteristic; (B) donation; (C) friction; (D) vengeance; (E) dress
165. **D**	**166. DISPEL** (A) rush; (B) alarm; (C) scatter; (D) amuse; (E) bewitch
275. **C**	**276. INTIMATE** (A) charm; (B) hint; (C) disguise; (D) frighten; (E) hum
385. **A**	**386. REBUFF** (A) deduct; (B) cancel; (C) snub; (D) return; (E) echo
495. **E**	**496. WAIVE** (A) exercise; (B) swing; (C) claim; (D) give up; (E) wear out
605. **C**	**606. BELLWETHER** (A) mythological giant; (B) weather forecaster; (C) leader of a flock; (D) thoughtless crowd
715. **D**	**716. CULPABLE** (A) deserving blame; (B) cultured; (C) imperfect; (D) excruciating
825. **A**	**826. FELICITY** (A) stealthiness; (B) congratulation; (C) aptness; (D) tenderness
935. **C**	**936. INTAGLIO** (A) complicated situation; (B) harem; (C) cameo; (D) engraving
1045. **C**	**1046. OBSOLETE** (A) common; (B) insensible; (C) immodest; (D) antiquated

1155. **A**	**1156. RANKLE** (A) fester; (B) explore; (C) rebuff; (D) declaim
1264. **D**	**1265. TRUNCATED** (A) abused; (B) lopped off; (C) sharpened to a fine point; (D) columnar
1373. **A**	**1374. CARTEL** (A) challenge; (B) position; (C) drawing; (D) phaeton; (E) denial
1482. **A**	**1483. ID** (A) alternate; (B) psychic agent; (C) calendar item; (D) essence
1591. **D**	**1592. PHAROS** (A) battle; (B) beacon; (C) spectre; (D) race; (E) vowel
1700. **C**	**1701. TROTH** (A) respite; (B) anger; (C) truth; (D) platitude; (E) deep red
1809. **B**	**1810. NECKLACE is to PEARLS as CHAIN is to** (A) metal; (B) prisoner; (C) locket; (D) silver; (E) links
1918. **A**	**1919. CAPTAIN : VESSEL : :** (A) guide : touring party; (B) boat : travel; (C) conductor : train; (D) conductor : orchestra; (E) musician : violin
2027. **C**	**2028. AWRY** (A) straight; (B) deplorable; (C) odd; (D) simple; (E) striking
2136. **A** *Page* 112	**2137. Our neighbor is so much disliked that we** **may well consider him a ————.** (A) pariah; (B) latitudinarian; (C) calumet; (D) cenotaph

56. A	**57. AUGER** (A) prediction; (B) weapon; (C) tool; (D) halo
166. C	**167. DISSEMINATE** (A) spread; (B) cluck; (C) disagree; (D) strip
276. B	**277. INTIMATED** (A) grew friendly; (B) denounced; (C) hinted; (D) frightened
386. C	**387. RECALCITRANT** (A) obedient; (B) defendant; (C) powder; (D) obstinate
496. D	**497. WANGLE** (A) moan; (B) mutilate; (C) exasperate; (D) manipulate; (E) triumph
606. C	**607. BENEDICT** (A) traitor; (B) small miracle; (C) prayer; (D) newly married man
716. A	**717. CUPIDITY** (A) veniality; (B) avarice; (C) coyness; (D) marksmanship
826. C	**827. FERAL** (A) iron-bearing; (B) panel; (C) wild; (D) violent
936. D	**937. INTEGUMENT** (A) burial; (B) will; (C) covering; (D) honesty
1046. D	**1047. OBTUSE** (A) blunt; (B) obscure; (C) complicated; (D) elephantine

1156. A	1157. RAPACIOUS (A) voracious; (B) dissolute; (C) jaunty; (D) zealous
1265. B	1266. TRUNCHEON (A) bone; (B) club; (C) beating; (D) cruelty
1374. A	1375. CATACHRESIS (A) misuse of words; (B) nervous disorder; (C) inhibition; (D) incompleteness
1483. B	1484. IDEOGRAPH (A) counterfeit; (B) mnemonic; (C) picture or symbol; (D) trade mark
1592. B	1593. PHOENIX (A) riddle; (B) amulet; (C) hedonist; (D) paragon; (E) monster
1701. C	1702. TUMID (A) moistened; (B) bombastic; (C) deflated; (D) polluted
1810. E	1811. SHOE is to LEATHER as HIGHWAY is to (A) passage; (B) road; (C) asphalt; (D) trail; (E) journey
1919. D	1920. FATHER : DAUGHTER : : (A) son : daughter; (B) son-in-law : daughter; (C) uncle : nephew; (D) uncle : aunt; (E) grandfather : mother
2028. A	2029. NEFARIOUS (A) clever; (B) necessary; (C) negligent; (D) short-sighted; (E) kindly
2137. A	2138. His ——— leads me to believe that he cannot be ———. (A) mendicity - injured; (B) mendacity - trusted; (C) catachresis - considered; (D) baldric - trained

57. **C**	**58. AUGMENT** (A) increase; (B) predict; (C) disclose; (D) challenge; (E) testify
167. **A**	**168. DISSENSION** (A) treatise; (B) pretense; (C) fear; (D) lineage; (E) discord
277. **C**	**278. INTREPID** (A) moist; (B) tolerant; (C) fearless; (D) rude; (E) gay
387. **D**	**388. RECANT** (A) intone; (B) disavow; (C) relate; (D) evaluate
497. **D**	**498. WARY** (A) dangerous; (B) cautious; (C) clear; (D) warm; (E) exciting
607. **D**	**608. BENIGNANT** (A) angry; (B) harmful; (C) ignorant; (D) kind
717. **B**	**718. CURSORY** (A) profane; (B) egregious; (C) superficial; (D) up-to-the-minute
827. **C**	**828. FETISH** (A) clan; (B) charm; (C) embryo; (D) shackle
937. **C**	**938. INTESTATE** (A) within the nation; (B) digestive; (C) without a will; (D) to swear publicly
1047. **A**	**1048. OBVIATE** (A) weigh; (B) object to; (C) violate; (D) remove

1157. A	**1158. RARA AVIS** (A) cynosure; (B) nonentity; (C) gourmet; (D) unusual person
1266. B	**1267. TURBID** (A) insubordinate; (B) distended; (C) hooded; (D) muddy
1375. A	**1376. CAT'S CRADLE** (A) a chess position; (B) a game played with a string; (C) a surgical instrument; (D) a rock formation
1484. C	**1485. ILLATIVE** (A) obscure; (B) contradictory; (C) illustrative; (D) inferential
1593. D	**1594. PICADOR** (A) small flute; (B) corsair; (C) matador's assistant; (D) type measure
1702. B	**1703. TUN** (A) entrance to an underground passage; (B) African drum; (C) reverberation; (D) large cask
1811. C	**1812. SERF is to FEUDALISM as** **ENTREPRENEUR is to** (A) laissez faire; (B) captain; (C) radical; (D) agriculture; (E) capitalism
1920. E	**1921. PISTOL : TRIGGER : :** (A) sword : holster; (B) dynamo : amperes; (C) motor : switch; (D) rifle : sight; (E) gun : race
2029. E	**2030. GLIB** (A) cheerful; (B) delightful; (C) dull; (D) quiet; (E) gloomy
2138. B	**2139. In Hindu mythology, ———— referred to** **a ———— to earth.** (A) autoclave - reference; (B) dipsomania - prayer; (C) divagation - bowing; (D) avatar - descent

| 58. | **59. AUDACIOUS** |
| A | (A) daring; (B) fearful; (C) indifferent; (D) attentive; (E) wicked |

| 168. | **169. DISSUADE** |
| E | (A) discharge; (B) discourage; (C) underrate; (D) convince; (E) lead astray |

| 278. | **279. INTRICATE** |
| C | (A) complicated; (B) fascinating; (C) medium; (D) human; (E) original |

| 388. | **389. RECIPROCAL** |
| B | (A) independent; (B) remorseful; (C) commercial; (D) international; (E) mutual |

| 498. | **499. WAXY** |
| B | (A) large; (B) serious; (C) cereous; (D) seric |

| 608. | **609. BENISON** |
| D | (A) approval; (B) blessing; (C) reward; (D) gift |

| 718. | **719. CURVILINEAR** |
| C | (A) surrounded by glass; (B) banked dangerously; (C) bounded by curved lines; (D) decorated excessively |

| 828. | **829. FETTLE** |
| B | (A) gala occasion; (B) shackle; (C) thriving condition; (D) part of a horse's leg |

| 938. | **939. INTERDICT** |
| C | (A) proclaim; (B) intervene; (C) reiterate; (D) forbid |

| 1048. | **1049. OCCLUDE** |
| D | (A) point out; (B) mystify; (C) close up; (D) allay |

1158. D	**1159. RAUCOUS** (A) fanatical; (B) impetuous; (C) headstrong; (D) hoarse
1267. D	**1268. TURGID** (A) distended; (B) muddy; (C) agitated; (D) sluggish
1376. B	**1377. CENSER** (A) army officer; (B) judge; (C) thurible; (D) assessor; (E) critic
1485. D	**1486. IMPLEACHED** (A) doomed; (B) foresworn; (C) interwoven; (D) blanched; (E) indicted
1594. C	**1595. PILASTER** (A) column; (B) lintel; (C) capital; (D) base
1703. D	**1704. UNCIAL** (A) relationship of uncle and nephew; (B) singleness; (C) a type of manuscript; (D) impenetrability
1812. E	**1813. FIN is to FISH as PROPELLER is to** (A) auto; (B) airplane; (C) grain elevator; (D) water; (E) bus
1921. C	**1922. CUBE : PYRAMID : :** (A) circle : triangle; (B) France : Egypt; (C) square : triangle; (D) cylinder : trylon; (E) hill : right angle
2030. D	**2031. PAUCITY** (A) lack; (B) ease; (C) hardship; (D) abundance; (E) stoppage
2139. D *Page* 118	**2140. An ———— study should reveal the influence of environment on man.** (A) ecumenical; (B) endemic; (C) ecological; (D) epigraphic

59. A	**60. AURA** (A) bitterness; (B) delight; (C) part of the ear; (D) prophet; (E) distinctive atmosphere
169. B	**170. DIVERGENCE** (A) annoyance; (B) difference; (C) entertainment; (D) distraction
279. A	**280. INVERSE** (A) opposite; (B) immovable; (C) remote; (D) progressive; (E) complicated
389. E	**390. RECOIL** (A) shrink; (B) attract; (C) electrify; (D) adjust; (E) enroll
499. C	**500. WILY** (A) graceful; (B) drooping; (C) cunning; (D) untamed; (E) nervous
609. B	**610. BESTIAL** (A) superior; (B) growling; (C) spiky; (D) brutal
719. C	**720. CYNOSURE** (A) easy task; (B) beacon; (C) inferior position; (D) rising star
829. C	**830. FEY** (A) appearing to be under a spell; (B) happy-go-lucky; (C) not clairvoyant; (D) lacking vision
939. D	**940. INTERNECINE** (A) pertaining to fraternal strife; (B) mutually destructive; (C) pertaining to sibling competition; (D) excessively diffident
1049. C	**1050. ODIUM** (A) remainder; (B) offensiveness; (C) music hall; (D) peculiarity

1159. **D**	**1160. RECALCITRANT** (A) calculating; (B) insubordinate; (C) cooperative; (D) delinquent
1268. **A**	**1269. TUTELARY** (A) shielding; (B) personal; (C) powerful; (D) nominal
1377. **C**	**1378. CEREMENT** (A) fortified chamber; (B) burial ceremony; (C) kind of pottery; (D) burial cloth
1486. **C**	**1487. IMPUDICITY** (A) insolence; (B) contentiousness; (C) immodesty; (D) shiftlessness
1595. **A**	**1596. PISMIRE** (A) grass seed; (B) demimonde; (C) filth; (D) ant
1704. **C**	**1705. UNCONSCIONABLE** (A) unrestrained; (B) immoral; (C) lethargic; (D) unreasonable
1813. **B**	**1814. PULP is to PAPER as HEMP is to** (A) rope; (B) baskets; (C) yarn; (D) cotton; (E) silk
1922. **C**	**1923. PROFIT : SELLING : :** (A) cost : price; (B) fame : bravery; (C) praying : loving; (D) medal : service; (E) money : work
2031. **D**	**2032. LUCRATIVE** (A) debasing; (B) fortunate; (C) influential; (D) monetary; (E) unprofitable
2140. **C**	**2141. The researcher in the field of ———— was** **interested in race improvement.** (A) euthenics; (B) euthanasia; (C) euphuism; (D) euphonics

60. E	**61. AUSPICES** (A) harshness; (B) protection; (C) admiration; (D) execution; (E) prediction
170. B	**171. DIVERSITY** (A) amusement; (B) discouragement; (C) variety; (D) mistrust; (E) confusion
280. A	**281. IPSO FACTO** (A) by that very fact; (B) made by hand; (C) according to him; (D) as a matter of fact
390. A	**391. REGIMEN** (A) troops; (B) administration; (C) record book; (D) province
500. C	**501. WRANGLE** (A) dispute; (B) come to grips; (C) squirm; (D) expel moisture; (E) plead
610. D	**611. BIBLIOPHILE** (A) lover of books; (B) student of the Bible; (C) librarian; (D) scribe
720. B	**721. DADO** (A) grotesque ornamentation; (B) musical composition; (C) prank or antic; (D) part of a pedestal
830. A	**831. FIAT** (A) failure; (B) authoritative command; (C) holiday outing; (D) pugnacity
940. A	**941. INTERPOLATE** (A) insert; (B) interchange; (C) secrete; (D) intersect
1050. B	**1051. OFFAL** (A) mud; (B) indecent behavior; (C) excrement; (D) animal waste

1160. B	**1161. RECIDIVIST** (A) one who receives; (B) one who relapses into criminality; (C) one who remains behind; (D) one who reciprocates
1269. A	**1270. TYMPANUM** (A) drum; (B) cymbal; (C) triangle; (D) cyclone
1378. D	**1379. CHAPMAN** (A) minister; (B) poet; (C) merchant; (D) teacher
1487. C	**1488. IMPUTATIVE** (A) attributing something discreditable to a person; (B) actuated by involuntary impulses; (C) exempt from punishment; (D) supposed
1596. D	**1597. PIZZICATO** (A) scanty; (B) delicate; (C) plucked; (D) allegretto
1705. D	**1706. UXORIOUS** (A) lavish in display; (B) clamorous; (C) doting on one's wife; (D) hating one's spouse
1814. A	**1815. SKIN is to MAN as HIDE is to** (A) scales; (B) fur; (C) animal; (D) hair; (E) fish
1923. B	**1924. BINDING : BOOK : :** (A) welding : tank; (B) chair : table; (C) wire : lamp; (D) pencil : paper; (E) glue : plate
2032. E	**2033. INDUBITABLE** (A) doubtless; (B) fraudulent; (C) honorable; (D) safe; (E) deniable
2141. A	**2142. ———— concerns itself with ———— of plants.** (A) etiology - eating; (B) ethnology - drying; (C) etiolation - blanching; (D) epistemology - collecting

61. **B**	**62. AUSTERITY** (A) heat; (B) displeasure; (C) honesty; (D) hospitableness; (E) sternness
171. **C**	**172. DOGGED** (A) obstinate; (B) sickly; (C) poetic; (D) honorable; (E) religious
281. **A**	**282. IRKSOME** (A) unreasonable; (B) unclean; (C) related; (D) aglow; (E) tedious
391. **B**	**392. RELINQUISH** (A) regret; (B) abandon; (C) pursue; (D) secure; (E) penetrate
501. **A**	**502. YEARN** (A) crave; (B) gape; (C) feel sleepy; (D) feel bored
611. **A**	**612. BIGOTED** (A) narrow-minded; (B) abusive; (C) loyal; (D) hypercritical
721. **D**	**722. DEBILITATE** (A) remove hair; (B) soothe; (C) argue vehemently; (D) weaken
831. **B**	**832. FIDUCIARY** (A) faithful; (B) speculative; (C) yielding interest; (D) holding in trust
941. **A**	**942. INTERSTICE** (A) crevice; (B) reciprocal action; (C) crossing; (D) insertion
1051. **D**	**1052. OMNISCIENT** (A) not illustrated; (B) exhilarated; (C) knowing all; (D) universal

1161. B	**1162. RECRUDESCENCE** (A) crudity; (B) degeneration; (C) resurgence; (D) retaliation
1270. A	**1271. TYRO** (A) novice; (B) autocrat; (C) veteran; (D) model
1379. C	**1380. CHEVY** (A) foster; (B) horse; (C) conceal; (D) chase; (E) fox
1488. A	**1489. INANITION** (A) emptiness; (B) heresy; (C) obsolescence; (D) disease
1597. C	**1598. PLAIN SONG** (A) modulation; (B) response; (C) motet; (D) psalm; (E) simple melody
1706. C	**1707. VARLETRY** (A) yeomanry; (B) feudal tenure; (C) retribution; (D) mob; (E) prophecy
1815. C	**1816. RAIN is to DROP as SNOW is to** (A) ice; (B) cold; (C) zero; (D) flake; (E) hail
1924. A	**1925. GYMNASIUM : HEALTH : :** (A) library : books; (B) books : study; (C) knowledge : school; (D) library : knowledge; (E) doctor : health
2033. E	**2034. SAVANT** (A) diplomat; (B) inventor; (C) moron; (D) thrifty person; (E) wiseacre
2142. C	**2143.** Through a ———— circumstance, we unexpectedly found ourselves on the same steamer with Uncle Harry. (A) fortuitous; (B) fetid; (C) friable; (D) lambent

62. E	63. AUTHORIZE (A) compose; (B) self-educate; (C) permit; (D) manage; (E) complicate
172. A	173. DOGMATIC (A) bovine; (B) canine; (C) opinionated; (D) unprincipled
282. E	283. IRRELEVANT (A) disrespectful; (B) tolerant; (C) sinful; (D) unrelated; (E) unresponsive
392. B	393. RELISH (A) destroy; (B) uphold; (C) defy; (D) associate; (E) enjoy
502. A	503. ZEALOT (A) breeze; (B) enthusiast; (C) vault; (D) wild animal; (E) musical instrument
612. A	613. BIBULOUS is used to describe (A) small curious objects of art; (B) scriptural style; (C) a person who collects books; (D) something which is absorbent
722. D	723. DECRY (A) discover; (B) delineate; (C) discredit; (D) profane
832. D	833. FILIGREE (A) fine thread; (B) narrow ribbon; (C) meat dish; (D) ornamental work
942. A	943. INTRANSIGENT (A) impassable; (B) irreconcilable; (C) harsh; (D) fly-by-night
1052. C	1053. ONEROUS (A) commendable; (B) single; (C) burdensome; (D) egotistic

1162. C	1163. **REDOLENT** (A) grief-stricken; (B) blushing; (C) fragrant; (D) poisonous
1271. A	1272. **UBIQUITOUS** (A) annoying; (B) metropolitan; (C) omnipresent; (D) evil
1380. D	1381. **CHRESTOMATHY** (A) anthology of plays; (B) collection of passages; (C) treasury of controversial essays; (D) literary concordance
1489. A	1490. **INCARNATE** (A) incestuous; (B) suffused; (C) embodied; (D) charmed; (E) meaty
1598. E	1599. **PLANKTON** (A) common weed; (B) minute animal or plant organisms; (C) light, four-wheeled carriage; (D) metal grips for climbing on ice
1707. D	1708. **VATICINAL** (A) prophetic; (B) vestigial; (C) prayerful; (D) neighborly
1816. D	1817. **RAISIN is to GRAPE as PRUNE is to** (A) apricot; (B) currant; (C) plum; (D) berry; (E) peach
1925. D	1926. **COKE : COAL : :** (A) bread : eat; (B) money : work; (C) bread : dough; (D) coal : rubber; (E) dough : wheat
2034. C	2035. **CONTENTIOUS** (A) appalling; (B) ingenious; (C) temperate; (D) agreeable
2143. A	2144. **I had a terrible night caused by an ——— during my sleep.** (A) epilogue; (B) insipidity; (C) insouciance; (D) incubus

63. C	**64. AUXILIARY** (A) greedy; (B) well-proportioned; (C) self-governing; (D) military; (E) assistant
173. C	**174. DOLDRUMS** (A) charity; (B) curing agents; (C) contagious disease; (D) low spirits; (E) places of safety
283. D	**284. JAMB** (A) part of doorway; (B) large crowd; (C) kind of fruit; (D) small animal
393. E	**394. RELUCTANT** (A) displeased; (B) stern; (C) conclusive; (D) voluntary; (E) unwilling
503. B	**504. ZEALOUS** (A) lazy; (B) enthusiastic; (C) envious; (D) careless
613. D	**614. BILLINGSGATE** (A) speech at the medieval English court; (B) coarse language; (C) insecure enclosure; (D) stevedore's hook
723. C	**724. DEFALCATE** (A) wither; (B) renovate; (C) embezzle; (D) question
833. D	**834. FLACCID** (A) liquid; (B) tough-fibred; (C) solid; (D) limp
943. B	**944. INVECTIVE** (A) electrical connector; (B) denunciation; (C) counsel; (D) assemblage
1053. C	**1054. OPPROBRIOUS** (A) disgraceful; (B) overwhelming; (C) resistant; (D) heretical

1163. C	**1164. REDOUBT** (A) homestead; (B) citadel; (C) supply dump; (D) sanctuary
1272. C	**1273. UMBRAGE** (A) resentment; (B) insult; (C) retribution; (D) encirclement
1381. B	**1382. CILIA** (A) aquatic animals; (B) eyelashes; (C) heavenly bodies; (D) swords
1490. C	**1491. INCHOATE** (A) imprecative; (B) saturnine; (C) scurrilous; (D) embryonic
1599. B	**1600. PLASHY** (A) rainy; (B) tawdry; (C) pretentious; (D) marshy
1708. A	**1709. VELLEITY** (A) sentimental weeping; (B) excusable error; (C) slight wish; (D) unfulfilled longing
1817. C	**1818. CONSTELLATION is to STAR as ARCHIPELAGO is to** (A) continent; (B) peninsula; (C) country; (D) island; (E) mono
1926. C	**1927. INDIAN : AMERICA : :** (A) Hindu : Hindustan; (B) wetback : Mexico; (C) soil : land; (D) magic : India; (E) Hindu : India
2035. D	**2036. INCIPIENT** (A) concluding; (B) dangerous; (C) hasty; (D) secret; (E) widespread
2144. D	**2145. The Romans depended on the ———— for the ———— of their homes.** (A) lares - protection; (B) caries - painting; (C) aborigines - blessing; (D) mores - erection

64. E	**65. AVERT** (A) prevent; (B) convince; (C) flee; (D) meet; (E) fear
174. D	**175. DOMESTIC** (A) internal; (B) alien; (C) untrained; (D) political; (E) beneficial
284. A	**285. JUGULAR** (A) trickier; (B) critical; (C) of the nervous system; (D) of the throat
394. E	**395. REMISS** (A) memorable; (B) neglectful; (C) useless; (D) prompt; (E) exact
504. B	**505. ZENITH** (A) lowest point; (B) compass; (C) summit; (D) middle; (E) wind direction
614. B	**615. BIVOUAC** (A) encamp; (B) erect tents; (C) light fires; (D) lay siege
724. C	**725. DEFALCATION** (A) disfigurement; (B) slander; (C) desertion; (D) misappropriation
834. D	**835. FLAGELLATE** (A) scold; (B) whip; (C) decorate; (D) scorn
944. B	**945. INVEIGH** (A) resentfully envy; (B) denounce; (C) sublimate; (D) outline parallels
1054. A	**1055. OPULENT** (A) inflamed; (B) rich; (C) fleeting; (D) disgorging pus

1164. B	**1165. REDOUBTABLE** (A) indisputable; (B) formidable; (C) indistinguishable; (D) impracticable
1273. A	**1274. UNDULATION** (A) heavy thud; (B) sensuous dancing; (C) careless manner; (D) wavelike motion
1382. B	**1383. CIRQUE** (A) harness; (B) cigar; (C) ring; (D) buckle; (E) breast plate
1491. D	**1492. INCUNABULA** (A) inner room; (B) shrines; (C) prophecies; (D) earliest stages; (E) immemorial mysteries
1600. D	**1601. PLEXUS** (A) terminal; (B) muscle; (C) cavity; (D) network
1709. C	**1710. VIABLE** (A) not excusable; (B) open to corrupt influence; (C) easily pulverized; (D) capable of living
1818. D	**1819. ACCOUNTANCY is to BOOKKEEPING as COURT REPORTING is to** (A) law; (B) judgment; (C) stenography; (D) lawyer; (E) judge
1927. E	**1928. WEALTH : MERCENARY : :** (A) fame : soldier; (B) love : mother; (C) gold : South Africa; (D) poverty : crime; (E) gold : Midas
2036. A	**2037. VIRILE** (A) honest; (B) loyal; (C) effeminate; (D) pugnacious; (E) virtuous
2145. A	**2146. In the study of grammatical forms, the ————— is very helpful.** (A) syllogism; (B) mattock; (C) paradigm; (D) pimpernel

65. A	**66. AVIARY** (A) avidity; (B) beehive; (C) hangar; (D) birdhouse
175. A	**176. DRASTIC** (A) indescribable; (B) theatrical; (C) radical; (D) stinging
285. D	**286. JOSTLE** (A) entertain; (B) travel afar; (C) crowd; (D) ride horseback; (E) deceive
395. B	**396. REMONSTRATE** (A) repine; (B) protest; (C) revere; (D) contort
505. C	**506. SYNONYMS** **More Difficult than the Previous Questions**
615. A	**616. BLATANT** (A) noisy; (B) fearless; (C) inflammable; (D) swollen
725. D	**726. DELETERIOUS** (A) spoiled; (B) raving; (C) gratifying; (D) harmful
835. B	**836. FLAMBOYANT** (A) inflamed; (B) cheerful; (C) ornate; (D) periodic
945. B	**946. INVETERATE** (A) confirmed; (B) inexperienced; (C) amateurish; (D) sapient
1055. B	**1056. ORDNANCE** (A) authoritative decree; (B) military supplies; (C) prescribed practice; (D) religious ceremony

1165. **B**	**1166. REFECTORY** (A) obstinate person; (B) dining hall; (C) penal institution; (D) radiance
1274. **D**	**1275. UNTOWARD** (A) fortunate; (B) peculiar; (C) irregular; (D) unfavorable
1383. **C**	**1384. CLOACA** (A) pretext; (B) sewer; (C) antiseptic; (D) armor
1492. **D**	**1493. INDEFEASIBLE** (A) not probable; (B) not justifiable; (C) not practicable; (D) not annullable
1601. **D**	**1602. PLINTH** (A) silver; (B) base; (C) apex; (D) wealth
1710. **D**	**1711. VIRIDESCENT** (A) pure; (B) green; (C) dizzy; (D) sturdy
1819. **C**	**1820. RUBBER is to FLEXIBILITY as STEEL is to** (A) iron; (B) copper; (C) pliability; (D) elasticity; (E) rigidity
1928. **E**	**1929. BOTTLE : BRITTLE : :** (A) tire : elastic; (B) rubber : flexible; (C) glass : transparent; (D) iron : strong; (E) chair : comfortable
2037. **C**	**2038. ASSIDUOUS** (A) courteous; (B) careless; (C) discouraged; (D) frank; (E) slow
2146. **C**	**2147. They had a wonderful view of the bay through the ————.** (A) nadir; (B) behemoth; (C) oriel; (D) fiat

66. D	**67. AVOWAL** (A) vacancy; (B) hobby; (C) desertion; (D) settled dislike; (E) open declaration
176. C	**177. DUBIOUS** (A) economical; (B) well-groomed; (C) boring; (D) discouraged; (E) uncertain
286. C	**287. LANGUID** (A) roundabout; (B) learned; (C) spiritless; (D) hidden; (E) praiseworthy
396. B	**397. REMORSEFUL** (A) deliberate; (B) sinful; (C) disinclined; (D) ungrateful; (E) regretful
	507. ABJECT (A) grammatical term; (B) reject; (C) despicable; (D) incorrect
616. A	**617. BLAZON** (A) flame; (B) display; (C) blare; (D) illuminate
726. D	**727. DEMAGOGUE** (A) inferior deity of Greece or Rome; (B) an unprincipled politician; (C) wooden statue; (D) large bottle
836. C	**837. FLAUNT** (A) disobey insolently; (B) mock; (C) escape; (D) display brazenly
946. A	**947. INVIDIOUS** (A) clandestine; (B) not visible; (C) offensive; (D) sapient
1056. B	**1057. ORIFICE** (A) aperture; (B) prayer; (C) position; (D) banner

1166. B	**1167. REFRACTORY** (A) perverse; (B) relating to a prior time; (C) pertaining to fractions; (D) nourishing
1275. D	**1276. URBANE** (A) rustic; (B) courteous; (C) poisonous; (D) papal
1384. B	**1385. CODICIL** (A) appendix; (B) will; (C) law; (D) classic
1493. D	**1494. INGLE** (A) sensation; (B) eskimo; (C) mold; (D) fireplace
1602. B	**1603. POLITY** (A) urbanity; (B) form of government; (C) crafty statesmanship; (D) party platform
1711. B	**1712. VOTARY** (A) proxy; (B) devotee; (C) elective office; (D) demagogue
1820. E	**1821. ABSENCE is to PRESENCE as STABLE is to** (A) steady; (B) secure; (C) safe; (D) changeable; (E) influential
1929. A	**1930. ELEPHANT : TUSK : :** (A) camel : hump; (B) leopard : skin; (C) knight : spear; (D) snake : fangs; (E) desk : top
2038. B	**2039. CATACLYSM** (A) blunder; (B) superstition; (C) treachery; (D) triumph; (E) status quo
2147. C	**2148. There is no reason to insult and ———— the man simply because you do not agree with him** (A) depict; (B) enervate; (C) defame; (D) distort

67. E	**68. BALUSTRADE** (A) banister; (B) ornament; (C) salon; (D) missile
177. E	**178. DURESS** (A) imprisonment; (B) permanence; (C) waste; (D) wheat
287. C	**288. LAUD** (A) praise; (B) cleanse; (C) replace; (D) squander; (E) frown upon
397. E	**398. REMUNERATION** (A) understanding; (B) finality; (C) indebtedness; (D) protest; (E) compensation
507. C	**508. ABJURE** (A) swear; (B) betray; (C) judge; (D) renounce
617. B	**618. BLENCH** (A) dredge; (B) clean; (C) shrink; (D) blow (as glass)
727. B	**728. DEMUR** (A) behave shyly; (B) object; (C) abandon; (D) intrude
837. D	**838. FLITCH** (A) marriage (colloquial); (B) torrent; (C) flank; (D) oath
947. C	**948. IRENIC** (A) easily angered; (B) sarcastic; (C) peaceable; (D) ferrous
1057. A	**1058. OROTUND** (A) ringing; (B) whirling; (C) corpulent; (D) embellished

1167. **A**	**1168. REGALE** (A) ennoble; (B) upbraid; (C) shout; (D) entertain
1276. **B**	**1277. VACUITY** (A) inanity; (B) leisure; (C) intrepidity; (D) indecision
1385. **A**	**1386. COEVAL** (A) malefactor; (B) pristine; (C) primordial; (D) future; (E) contemporary
1494. **D**	**1495. INSENSATE** (A) undefiled; (B) brutish; (C) wrathful; (D) taciturn
1603. **B**	**1604. POLTERGEIST** (A) coward; (B) ghost; (C) counterirritant; (D) goose
1712. **B**	**1713. WARLOCK** (A) witch; (B) mortar; (C) wizard; (D) enmity
1821. **D**	**1822. SAFETY VALVE is to BOILER as FUSE is to** (A) motor; (B) house; (C) wire; (D) city; (E) factory
1930. **D**	**1931. CAUSEWAY : BRIDGE : :** (A) swamp : stream; (B) viaduct : land; (C) bridge : river; (D) train : road; (E) low : high
2039. **E**	**2040. AUSPICIOUS** (A) condemnatory; (B) conspicuous; (C) unfavorable; (D) questionable; (E) spicy
2148. **C**	**2149. Through his ————, he deceived us all.** (A) whit; (B) selvage; (C) canard; (D) petard

68. A	**69. BARBARITY** (A) tonsure; (B) brutality; (C) nudity; (D) insanity
178. A	**179. DUTIFUL** (A) lasting; (B) sluggish; (C) required; (D) soothing; (E) obedient
288. A	**289. LESSEE** (A) lender; (B) giver; (C) receiver; (D) renter
398. E	**399. RENEGADE** (A) deserter; (B) hermit; (C) yardstick; (D) king
508. D	**509. ABLUTION** (A) abolition; (B) cleansing; (C) bleeding; (D) bliss
618. C	**619. BOMBAST** (A) inflated style; (B) steadying influence; (C) loud noise; (D) cannon
728. B	**729. DENIGRATE** (A) defame; (B) contradict; (C) digress; (D) repudiate
838. C	**839. FLOTSAM** (A) flower; (B) wreckage; (C) water; (D) moth
948. C	**949. IRASCIBLE** (A) shameless; (B) fortuitous; (C) choleric; (D) tedious
1058. A	**1059. ORTHOGRAPHY** (A) beautiful handwriting; (B) correct spelling; (C) autobiography; (D) illegibility

1168. **D**	**1169. RENASCENT** (A) reborn; (B) current; (C) statutory; (D) reformed
1277. **A**	**1278. VACUOUS** (A) vain; (B) misleading; (C) stupid; (D) fantastic
1386. **E**	**1387. COLLIGATE** (A) bind; (B) bark; (C) educate; (D) collide
1495. **B**	**1496. INSPISSATED** (A) animated; (B) thickened; (C) attenuated; (D) mixed thoroughly
1604. **B**	**1605. PORTENTOUS** (A) ostentatious; (B) presumptive; (C) oppressive; (D) prodigious
1713. **C**	**1714. WEN** (A) gall; (B) sebaceous tumor; (C) naval winch; (D) antique bric-a-brac
1822. **A**	**1823. SCHOLARLY is to UNSCHOLARLY as** **LEARNED is to** (A) ignorant; (B) wise; (C) skilled; (D) scholarly; (E) literary
1931. **A**	**1932. HACK : DRIVER : :** (A) buggy : horse; (B) ship : crew; (C) machine : operator; (D) tug : pilot; (E) school : teacher
2040. **C**	**2041. BANTER** (A) conversation; (B) criticism; (C) gossip; (D) irony; (E) serious talk
2149. **C**	**2150. The lover of democracy has an ————** **toward totalitarianism.** (A) antipathy; (B) empathy; (C) antipode; (D) idiopathy

69. B	**70. BEFIT** (A) assist; (B) suit; (C) slander; (D) stretch; (E) effect
179. E	**180. DWINDLE** (A) hang loosely; (B) deceive; (C) fight; (D) share; (E) decrease
289. D	**290. LETHAL** (A) belated; (B) deadly; (C) neglectful; (D) devout; (E) oblivious
399. A	**400. REPRISAL** (A) retaliation; (B) drawing; (C) capture; (D) release; (E) suspicion
509. B	**510. ABNEGATION** (A) renunciation; (B) failure to conform to rule; (C) utter humiliation; (D) sudden departure
619. A	**620. BOONDOGGLE** (A) delay by filibustering; (B) pretend to be ill; (C) try to commit sabotage; (D) do useless work
729. A	**730. DENIZEN** (A) criminal; (B) frequenter of squalid retreats; (C) inhabitant; (D) deep-water fish
839. B	**840. FLOUT** (A) display; (B) insult; (C) violate; (D) cheat
949. C	**950. IRREFRAGABLE** (A) irrefutable; (B) unbreakable; (C) irrespectful; (D) irreverent
1059. B	**1060. OSCULATE** (A) record electrically; (B) waver; (C) intensify; (D) kiss

1169. A	1170. RENEGADE (A) petty officer; (B) celebration; (C) new arrival; (D) deserter
1278. C	1279. VAGARY (A) wanderer; (B) whim; (C) emptiness; (D) laxity
1387. A	1388. COLOPHON (A) palimpsest; (B) antithesis; (C) emblem; (D) manuscript; (E) bombast
1496. B	1497. INTERCALATION (A) calcification; (B) altercation; (C) intervention; (D) insertion
1605. D	1606. POTSHERD (A) primitive agricultural implement; (B) herdsman; (C) fragment of earthen pot; (D) caretaker
1714. B	1715. WHILOM (A) old-fashioned; (B) intermittent; (C) quondam; (D) quaint
1823. A	1824. IMMIGRANT is to ARRIVAL as EMIGRATION is to (A) leaving; (B) alien; (C) native; (D) Italian; (E) emigrant
1932. D	1933. CONVEX : CONCAVE : : (A) in : out; (B) nose : mouth; (C) hill : hole; (D) round : square; (E) myopia : astigmatism
2041. E	2042. VERNACULAR (A) literary speech; (B) correct usage; (C) long words; (D) oratory; (E) poetic style
2150. A	2151. An ———— may connect the names of members of a partnership. (A) addendum; (B) ampersand; (C) epigram; (D) encomium

70. B	**71. BELLIGERENT** (A) worldly; (B) warlike; (C) loud-mouthed; (D) furious; (E) artistic
180. E	**181. EDICT** (A) abbreviation; (B) lie; (C) carbon copy; (D) correction; (E) decree
290. B	**291. LETHARGY** (A) insensibility; (B) death; (C) freedom; (D) generosity
400. A	**401. REPUDIATE** (A) hail; (B) support; (C) start; (D) disown; (E) duplicate
510. A	**511. ABORTIVE** (A) decadent; (B) failing to succeed; (C) carrying off surreptitiously; (D) degrading
620. D	**621. BOTCH** (A) baking; (B) bungle; (C) quantity of dough; (D) ink stain
730. C	**731. DEPRECATE** (A) mar; (B) deplete; (C) destroy partially; (D) disapprove
840. B	**841. FLUME** (A) gorge; (B) fish; (C) trash; (D) blaze
950. A	**951. ITINERANT** (A) journeying; (B) pronged; (C) tinting; (D) begging
1060. D	**1061. OTIOSE** (A) long-winded; (B) thick-skinned; (C) inactive; (D) hateful

1170. **D**	**1171. REPRISE** (A) information; (B) repetition; (C) recollection; (D) reformation
1279. **B**	**1280. VALETUDINARIAN** (A) physician; (B) man-servant; (C) invalid; (D) speaker
1388. **C**	**1389. COMMONALTY** (A) common people; (B) wasteland; (C) autonomy; (D) public welfare; (E) platitude
1497. **D**	**1498. INTERPELLATE** (A) clarify; (B) alter by inserting; (C) admonish; (D) question formally
1606. **C**	**1607. POUNDAL** (A) unit of force; (B) reverberation; (C) iteration; (D) monetary unit
1715. **C**	**1716. WHIPSAW** (A) put in a dilemma; (B) vacillate; (C) effect by indirect means; (D) to worst in two ways at once
1824. **A**	**1825. GOVERNOR is to STATE as GENERAL is to** (A) lieutenant; (B) navy; (C) army; (D) captain; (E) admiral
1933. **C**	**1934. PRISM : KALEIDOSCOPE : :** (A) window : house; (B) bottle : glass; (C) tool : toy; (D) gear : machine; (E) sight : play
2042. **A**	**2043. EMOLUMENT** (A) capital; (B) penalty; (C) liabilities; (D) loss; (E) output
2151. **B** *Page* 142	**2152. A ——— person cannot be expected to** **resist ———.** (A) profligate - money; (B) raucous - temptation; (C) recreant - aggression; (D) squalid - quarreling

71. B	**72. BENEVOLENCE** (A) good fortune; (B) well-being; (C) inheritance; (D) violence; (E) charitableness
181. E	**182. EFFIGY** (A) fire; (B) ceremony; (C) image; (D) consequence
291. A	**292. LIAISON** (A) permission; (B) laziness; (C) tie; (D) scarf
401. D	**402. REPUGNANT** (A) distasteful; (B) irritable; (C) regretful; (D) honored; (E) restful
511. B	**512. ABRADE** (A) plait; (B) bake; (C) apologize; (D) scrape; (E) break
621. B	**622. BOWDLERIZE** (A) ratiocinate; (B) interpolate; (C) asseverate; (D) expurgate
731. D	**732. DEROGATE** (A) disparage; (B) dismiss; (C) disinherit; (D) discharge
841. A	**842. FLUMMERY** (A) finery; (B) treachery; (C) scoffing remark; (D) humbug
951. A	**952. JADED** (A) eager; (B) hungry; (C) bored; (D) dulled
061. C	**1062. PALADIN** (A) sedan chair; (B) precious metal; (C) legendary hero; (D) evil genie

1171. B	**1172. RESILIENT** (A) sparkling; (B) elastic; (C) spongy; (D) clinging
1280. C	**1281. VANGUARD** (A) leaders; (B) fighters; (C) defenders; (D) movers
1389. A	**1390. COMPLINE** (A) morning prayer; (B) last service; (C) spline; (D) rubric; (E) antiphonal
1498. D	**1499. INUTILE** (A) unaccustomed; (B) unprofitable; (C) toughen; (D) lacking in civility
1607. A	**1608. PRESIDIUM** (A) ruling cabinet minister; (B) chief of secret police; (C) administrative committee; (D) presiding officer
1716. D	**1717. WIMBLE** (A) bore; (B) sink; (C) sew; (D) weep; (E) scold
1825. C	**1826. LETTER CARRIER is to MAIL as** **MESSENGER is to** (A) value; (B) dispatches; (C) easy; (D) complicated; (E) fast
1934. D	**1935. MARTINET : STOIC : :** (A) soldier : bravery; (B) general : philosopher; (C) man : boy; (D) sergeant : general; (E) strict : hard
2043. B	**2044. TURGID** (A) dusty; (B) muddy; (C) rolling; (D) deflated; (E) tense
2152. C	**2153. He hated his father so intensely that he** **committed ————.** (A) parricide; (B) fratricide; (C) genocide; (D) matricide

72. E	73. BENIGN (A) contagious; (B) fatal; (C) ignorant; (D) kindly; (E) decorative
182. C	183. ELITE (A) great joy; (B) older generation; (C) legendary kingdom; (D) choice part; (E) body of voters
292. C	293. LITHE (A) tough; (B) obstinate; (C) flexible; (D) damp; (E) gay
402. A	403. RESCIND (A) cancel; (B) renew; (C) divide; (D) pave; (E) demand
512. D	513. ABROGATE (A) abdicate; (B) denounce; (C) abolish; (D) dissemble
622. D	623. BRAHMIN (A) water carrier; (B) tea canister; (C) pedant; (D) Oriental conveyance
732. A	733. DEROGATION (A) inquiry; (B) detraction; (C) roguery; (D) reformation
842. D	843. FOIST (A) raise over the head; (B) expose to the public; (C) founder in shallow water; (D) pass off as genuine
952. D	953. JEJUNE (A) flourishing; (B) interesting; (C) insipid; (D) youthful
1062. C	1063. PALLED (A) cloyed; (B) shocked; (C) pierced; (D) weighted

1172. B	**1173. RESTIVE** (A) patient; (B) immovable; (C) refractory; (D) recuperative
1281. A	**1282. VAPID** (A) gaseous; (B) inane; (C) speedy; (D) boastful; (E) loving
1390. B	**1391. CONGENERIC** (A) remotely related; (B) artificially reproduced; (C) carefree in nature; (D) of the same kind
1499. B	**1500. JALOUSIE** (A) landscape; (B) shutter; (C) cart; (D) temperament
1608. C	**1609. PROSTHESIS** (A) attempt to convert; (B) addition of an artificial part to the human body; (C) complete exhaustion; (D) figure of speech
1717. A	**1718. WINKLE** (A) head covering; (B) snail; (C) blinder; (D) shop
1826. B	**1827. CLOTH is to COAT as GINGHAM is to** (A) doll; (B) cover; (C) washable; (D) dress; (E) dressmaker
1935. E	**1936. CADAVER : ANIMAL : :** (A) salad : greens; (B) corpse : man; (C) death : life; (D) morgue : jungle; (E) life : death
2044. D	**2045. EXPUNGE** (A) clarify; (B) cleanse; (C) perpetuate; (D) investigate; (E) underline
2153. A *Page* 146	**2154. Being very ————, he knew what was going on about him.** (A) circumlocutory; (B) choleric; (C) caustic; (D) circumspect

73. D	74. BERATE (A) classify; (B) scold; (C) underestimate; (D) take one's time; (E) evaluate
183. D	184. ELUDE (A) expel; (B) impress; (C) rob; (D) evade; (E) keep
293. C	294. LITIGATION (A) designation; (B) challenge; (C) judicial contest; (D) condemnation
403. A	404. RESIDUE (A) remainder; (B) evaporation; (C) rent; (D) admission; (E) payment
513. C	514. ABSOLVE (A) bless; (B) exculpate; (C) melt; (D) repent
623. C	624. BRAKE (A) thicket; (B) ravine; (C) clearing; (D) grove
733. B	734. DESCRIED (A) rebuffed; (B) hailed; (C) recalled; (D) sighted
843. D	844. FOMENT (A) sour; (B) incite; (C) prepare; (D) array
953. C	954. JEOPARDY (A) crime; (B) offense; (C) danger; (D) disagreement
1063. A	1064. PALLIATE (A) celebrate; (B) fade; (C) bury; (D) alleviate

1173. C	**1174. RETRENCH** (A) excavate; (B) reply; (C) refuse; (D) economize
1282. B	**1283. VATICINATE** (A) prophesy; (B) hesitate; (C) pacify; (D) verify
1391. D	**1392. CORYPHÉE** (A) harbinger; (B) caryatid; (C) odalisk; (D) ballet dancer
1500. B	**1501. JANISSARY** (A) Knight Templar; (B) Turkish soldier; (C) custodian; (D) crusader
1609. B	**1610. PROTEAN** (A) nutritious; (B) mighty; (C) variable; (D) exemplary
1718. B	**1719. XENOPHOBIC** (A) susceptible to disease; (B) opposed to gambling; (C) hating or fearing strangers; (D) hating or fearful of dogs
1827. D	**1828. BOAT is to DOCK as AIRPLANE is to** (A) wing; (B) strut; (C) engine; (D) wind; (E) hangar
1936. B	**1937. MORPHINE : PAIN : :** (A) symptom : illness; (B) doctor : relief; (C) dope : addict; (D) eraser : spot; (E) hope : relief
2045. C	**2046. PANORAMIC** (A) brilliant; (B) pinpoint; (C) pretty; (D) fluorescent; (E) unique
2154. D	**2155. The convicted man resorted to ———— in attacking his accusers.** (A) nepotism; (B) anathema; (C) panoply; (D) bravura

74. B	**75. BRUNT** (A) mistake; (B) tact; (C) swine; (D) force; (E) scald
184. D	**185. ELUSIVE** (A) helpful; (B) baffling; (C) abundant; (D) lessening; (E) expanding
294. C	**295. LOATH** (A) idle; (B) worried; (C) unwilling; (D) ready; (E) sad
404. A	**405. RESOLUTELY** (A) fully; (B) briefly; (C) firmly; (D) finally; (E) calmly
514. B	**515. ABSTEMIOUS** (A) lacking a stalk; (B) bubbling; (C) temperate; (D) bitter to the taste
624. A	**625. BRIGAND** (A) pirate vessel; (B) guardhouse; (C) officer; (D) bandit
734. D	**735. DESICCATE** (A) loathe; (B) completely destroy; (C) violate; (D) make dry
844. B	**845. FORENSIC** (A) agreeable; (B) exotic; (C) logical; (D) argumentative
954. C	**955. JEREMIAD** (A) dolorous tirade; (B) optimistic prophecy; (C) prolonged journey; (D) religious pilgrimage
1064. D	**1065. PALLIATIVE** (A) soporific; (B) pernicious; (C) adulterant; (D) softening

1174. D	**1175. RETRIBUTION** (A) levy; (B) retaliation; (C) regret; (D) mutual admiration
1283. A	**1284. VAUNTING** (A) boasting; (B) pretending; (C) flattering; (D) leaping
1392. D	**1393. COSSET** (A) drink mildly; (B) deceive; (C) pamper; (D) fit closely
1501. B	**1502. JARDINIERE** (A) professional soldier; (B) large flowerpot; (C) female gardener; (D) beekeeper
1610. C	**1611. PROVENANCE** (A) place of origin; (B) foresight; (C) scion's inheritance; (D) provisions
1719. C	**1720. YAPP** (A) an outcry; (B) a style of bookbinding; (C) a small vessel; (D) an oriental
1828. E	**1829. OAT is to BUSHEL as DIAMOND is to** (A) gram; (B) hardness; (C) usefulness; (D) carat; (E) ornament
1937. D	**1938. POLYMER : CELL : :** (A) chain : link; (B) fibre : plastic; (C) coin : money; (D) chemistry : elements; (E) food : wheat
2046. B	**2047. IGNOMINY** (A) fame; (B) isolation; (C) misfortune; (D) sorrow; (E) stupidity
2155. B *Page* 150	**2156. The ———— woman was the ———— of** all eyes. (A) titled - cupola; (B) lonely - sinecure; (C) ugly - doggerel; (D) attractive - cynosure

75. D	**76. BICAMERAL** (A) dealing with life forms; (B) meeting on alternate years; (C) over-sweet; (D) having two legislative branches; (E) having two meanings
185. B	**186. EMULATE** (A) mail; (B) drive; (C) rival; (D) complain
295. C	**296. LOQUACIOUS** (A) grim; (B) stern; (C) talkative; (D) lighthearted; (E) liberty-loving
405. C	**406. RESOURCES** (A) debts; (B) liabilities; (C) funds; (D) losses
515. C	**516. ACANTHUS** (A) leaf-like architectural ornamentation; (B) gummy substance used in stiffening fabrics; (C) ethereal spirit; (D) ornamental vessel
625. D	**626. BROACH** (A) criticize; (B) venture to approach; (C) introduce as topic of conversation; (D) decorate
735. D	**736. DESIDERATUM** (A) something desired; (B) minor consideration; (C) petition; (D) bequest
845. D	**846. FORTITUDE** (A) aggressiveness; (B) success; (C) endurance; (D) completion
955. A	**956. JETTISON** (A) jeopardize; (B) assault; (C) fasten; (D) discard
1065. D	**1066. PALTER** (A) trifle; (B) hesitate; (C) disrupt; (D) wail

1175. B	1176. REVENANT (A) dream; (B) relation; (C) tax; (D) apparition
1284. A	1285. VENAL (A) corruptible; (B) vein-like; (C) airy; (D) alcoholic
1393. C	1394. CRENELATION (A) injury; (B) battlement; (C) material; (D) crowning; (E) crew
1502. B	1503. JIHAD (A) outcry; (B) lament; (C) prayer; (D) crusade; (E) procession
1611. A	1612. PSALTERY (A) kneeling bench; (B) sacred song; (C) musical instrument; (D) synagogue
1720. B	1721. ZEUGMA (A) caret; (B) solecism; (C) zombi; (D) wasteland
1829. D	1830. PHYSIOLOGY is to SCIENCE as LAW is to (A) jurist; (B) court; (C) profession; (D) contract; (E) suit
1938. A	1939. MACAROON : ALMOND : : (A) cake : dough; (B) mint : flavor; (C) vanilla : bean; (D) fudge : molasses; (E) bread : wheat
2047. A	2048. RELEVANT (A) ingenious; (B) inspiring; (C) obvious; (D) inappropriate; (E) tentative
2156. D *Page* 152	2157. A ———— is likely to give you the wrong advice. (A) nuance; (B) panacea; (C) charlatan; (D) virago

76. **D**	**77. BIPARTISAN** (A) adhering to views of one party; (B) prejudiced; (C) representing two parties; (D) bisected; (E) narrow
186. **C**	**187. ENIGMATIC** (A) sarcastic; (B) skillful; (C) puzzling; (D) healthy; (E) like an insect
296. **C**	**297. LUCRATIVE** (A) painful; (B) creditable; (C) preferential; (D) profitable
406. **C**	**407. RESPITE** (A) feud; (B) receipt; (C) flattery; (D) teasing; (E) lull
516. **A**	**517. ACCRUE** (A) translate; (B) cut short; (C) store up; (D) be added
626. **C**	**627. BROMIDIC** (A) hypothetical; (B) banal; (C) effervescent; (D) purgative
736. **A**	**737. DESUETUDE** (A) spasmodic action; (B) languor induced by hot weather; (C) disuse; (D) harmlessness
846. **C**	**847. FORTUITOUS** (A) happy; (B) tending to strengthen; (C) valiant; (D) accidental
956. **D**	**957. JOCOSE** (A) warlike; (B) jesting; (C) stout; (D) red-faced
1066. **A**	**1067. PANACEA** (A) remedy; (B) honor; (C) omelet; (D) sickness

1176. D	**1177. RIBALD** (A) indecent; (B) teasing; (C) noisy; (D) quarrelsome
1285. A	**1286. VENIAL** (A) excusable; (B) likeable; (C) salable; (D) corruptible
1394. B	**1395. CUTCHERRY** (A) courthouse; (B) beach plum; (C) spice; (D) carpenter's tool
1503. D	**1504. KESTREL** (A) renegade; (B) small falcon; (C) sadiron; (D) diffident
1612. C	**1613. PULLULATE** (A) multiply; (B) divide; (C) supplicate; (D) swell
1721. B	**1722. ANALOGIES** *Directions:* The first two words are related to each other. Find the relationship, and then decide which word is related in the same way to the third word.
1830. C	**1831. HUNGER is to INSTINCT as IMAGINATION is to** (A) ideal; (B) mind; (C) thought; (D) image
1939. D	**1940. INTEGER : DECIMAL : :** (A) 100 : 10; (B) 1 : 0; (C) decimal : fraction; (D) whole number : fraction; (E) 100 : per cent
2048. D	**2049. APPOSITE** (A) irrelevant; (B) contrary; (C) different; (D) spontaneous; (E) tricky
2157. C	**2158. The ———— professor put his wife out and went to sleep with the cat.** (A) diurnal; (B) distrait; (C) dubious; (D) dilatory

77. C	78. BIZARRE (A) accurate; (B) solvent; (C) mart; (D) fantastic
187. C	188. ENMESH (A) entangle; (B) oppose; (C) organize; (D) challenge; (E) respond
297. D	298. LUDICROUS (A) profitable; (B) excessive; (C) disordered; (D) ridiculous; (E) undesirable
407. E	408. RESTIVE (A) permanent; (B) quiet; (C) sullen; (D) impatient
517. D	518. ACHROMATIC (A) without color; (B) timeless; (C) not musical; (D) involuntary
627. B	628. BROOK (A) prevent; (B) defy; (C) tolerate; (D) assist
737. C	738. DESULTORY (A) shy; (B) torrid; (C) cautious; (D) aimless
847. D	848. FOURTH ESTATE (A) underprivileged minority; (B) judicial system; (C) newspaper profession; (D) business world
957. B	958. JOIST (A) bump; (B) tilt; (C) knot; (D) beam
1067. A	1068. PANEGYRIC (A) frenzied petition; (B) abusive oration; (C) encomium; (D) demagogic utterance

1177. **A**	**1178. RIPOSTE** (A) attack; (B) disintegration; (C) shore line; (D) repartee
1286. **A**	**1287. VENTRAL** (A) draughty; (B) abdominal; (C) thoracic; (D) nasal
1395. **A**	**1396. DAEDAL** (A) obdurate; (B) ineffable; (C) prostrate; (D) skillful
1504. **B**	**1505. LACHES** (A) streamlets; (B) bolts; (C) wound; (D) neglect
1613. **A**	**1614. PUNCHEON** (A) pot-bellied person; (B) puppet show; (C) wooden mallet; (D) large cask
1722.	**1723. SOPRANO is to HIGH as BASS is to** (A) violin; (B) good; (C) low; (D) fish; (E) soft
1831. **B**	**1832. CAPTAIN is to VESSEL as DIRECTOR is to** (A) touring party; (B) board; (C) travel; (D) orchestra; (E) musician
1940. **D**	**1941. STOCK : BOND : :** (A) owner : lender; (B) inventory : merchandise; (C) word : promise; (D) security : price; (E) equity : interest
2049. **A**	**2050. AMBULATORY** (A) confined to bed; (B) able to walk; (C) injured; (D) quarantined; (E) suffering from disease
2158. **B**	**2159. Art is long and time is ———.** (A) fervid; (B) fallow; (C) nebulous; (D) evanescent

78. **D**	**79. BLAND** (A) gentle; (B) guilty; (C) salty; (D) unfinished; (E) majestic
188. **A**	**189. ENMITY** (A) boredom; (B) puzzle; (C) offensive language; (D) ill will; (E) entanglement
298. **D**	**299. MACERATE** (A) waste away; (B) construct; (C) shape up; (D) mob
408. **D**	**409. RETROSPECT** (A) withdrawal; (B) review of the past; (C) very severe punishment; (D) prediction; (E) self-examination
518. **A**	**519. ACRIMONIOUS** (A) harmonious; (B) debatable; (C) caustic; (D) loud
628. **C**	**629. BRUSQUE** (A) keen; (B) abrupt; (C) menacing; (D) quick
738. **D**	**739. DETRITUS** (A) criticism; (B) obsolescence; (C) debris; (D) analgesic
848. **C**	**849. FRACTIOUS** (A) bent; (B) weak; (C) peevish; (D) redolent
958. **D**	**959. JUNTO** (A) dessert; (B) convivial excursion; (C) second-hand store; (D) faction
1068. **C**	**1069. PANOPLY** (A) comprehensive survey; (B) full suit of armor; (C) overhanging projection; (D) elaborate display

1178. D	1179. RISIBLE (A) capable of elevation; (B) irritable; (C) pertaining to laughter; (D) alert
1287. B	1288. VERTIGINOUS (A) magnetic; (B) upright; (C) giddy; (D) green
1396. D	1397. DAVIT (A) imprecation; (B) sworn statement; (C) crane; (D) oarlock
1505. D	1506. LACTEAL (A) milky; (B) mysterious; (C) secretive; (D) pertaining to tear glands
1614. D	1615. QUIDDITY (A) oddity; (B) essence; (C) quittance; (D) quietus
1723. C	1724. OLFACTORY is to NOSE as TACTILE is to (A) tacit; (B) bloody; (C) finger; (D) handkerchief; (E) stomach
1832. D	1833. ADUMBRATE is to FORESHADOW as DECLINE is to (A) increase; (B) decrease; (C) stultify; (D) stupefy
1941. E	1942. HYGROMETER : BAROMETER : : (A) water : mercury; (B) snow : rain; (C) humidity : pressure; (D) temperature : weather; (E) forecast : rain
2050. A	2051. DISPARAGE (A) applaud; (B) degrade; (C) erase; (D) reform; (E) scatter
2159. D	2160. The ————— flower was also —————. (A) pretty - redolent; (B) dropping - potable; (C) pale - opulent; (D) blooming - amenable

79. A	**80. BLITHE** (A) wicked; (B) criminal; (C) merry; (D) unintelligible; (E) substantial
189. D	**190. ENSUE** (A) compel; (B) remain; (C) absorb; (D) plead; (E) follow
299. A	**300. MAESTRO** (A) official; (B) ancestor; (C) teacher; (D) watchman; (E) alien
409. B	**410. REVELATION** (A) respect; (B) disclosure; (C) repetition; (D) suitability; (E) remainder
519. C	**520. ACRIMONY** (A) deceit; (B) rattling; (C) sharpness; (D) accusation
629. B	**630. BRUSQUERIE** (A) wooded area; (B) cordiality; (C) boorishness; (D) rotisserie
739. C	**740. DICHOTOMY** (A) cutting in two; (B) ambiguous expression; (C) tendency to digress; (D) double entendre
849. C	**850. FROND** (A) forehead; (B) front; (C) herd; (D) leaf
959. D	**960. KELP** (A) military cap; (B) sharp cry; (C) disembodied spirit; (D) seaweed ash
1069. B	**1070. PARIAH** (A) priest; (B) venerable ancestor; (C) outcast; (D) one with magic power

1179. C	1180. ROCOCO (A) foolish; (B) florid; (C) fiery; (D) simple
1288. C	1289. VICARIOUS (A) substituted; (B) neighborly; (C) self-imposed; (D) imaginary
1397. C	1398. DEBOUCH (A) pour gently; (B) divert; (C) seduce; (D) emerge
1506. A	1507. LAGNIAPPE (A) something given a customer "for good measure"; (B) gouache; (C) savory; (D) work of cutting precious stones
1615. B	1616. QUIRT (A) riding-whip; (B) witty remark; (C) idiosyncrasy; (D) bludgeon
1724. C	1725. STREET is to HORIZONTAL as BUILDING is to (A) tall; (B) brick; (C) broad; (D) vertical; (E) large
1833. B	1834. APOGEE is to PERIGEE as APPOSITE is to (A) inappropriate; (B) opposite; (C) composite; (D) paradoxical
1942. C	1943. NEGOTIABLE : CHECK : : (A) frozen : asset; (B) inventory : merchandise; (C) bank : money; (D) trade : tariff; (E) flowing : water
2051. A	2052. LIMPID (A) calm; (B) turbid; (C) crippled; (D) delightful; (E) sad
2160. A	2161. The ———— effects of the drug made her very sleepy. (A) succinct; (B) spurious; (C) soporific; (D) supine

80. C	81. BOLSTER (A) contradict; (B) insist; (C) defy; (D) sleep; (E) prop
190. E	191. ENTERPRISING (A) enrolling; (B) commercial; (C) amusing; (D) containing; (E) venturesome
300. C	301. MAGNANIMOUS (A) high-minded; (B) faithful; (C) concerned; (D) individual; (E) small
410. B	411. REVERBERATE (A) uncover; (B) blame; (C) resound; (D) regain; (E) restore to life
520. C	521. ADUMBRATE (A) thunder; (B) confuse; (C) outline; (D) deploy carefully
630. C	631. BUCOLIC (A) hymn-like; (B) unripened; (C) pastoral; (D) doltish
740. A	741. DIDACTIC (A) rhythmic; (B) broken; (C) divided; (D) instructive
850. D	851. FROWARD (A) complaisant; (B) perverse; (C) candid; (D) precocious
960. D	961. KIOSK (A) monolithic column; (B) ancient musical instrument; (C) news-stand or outdoor stall; (D) small hill or elevation
1070. C	1071. PARLEY (A) grain; (B) volley; (C) conference; (D) stop; (E) travel

1180. B	**1181. ROOK** (A) corner; (B) cross; (C) cheat; (D) unit of measure
1289. A	**1290. VIRAGO** (A) bacillus; (B) bombast; (C) wanton; (D) shrew
1398. D	**1399. DECIDUOUS** (A) transitory; (B) stubborn; (C) paleolithic; (D) staining
1507. A	**1508. LAMBENT** (A) bright; (B) cool; (C) flickering; (D) diffused
1616. A	**1617. QUONDAM** (A) which was to be done; (B) having been formerly; (C) to this extent; (D) cited as an authority
1725. D	**1726. PREDICAMENT is to CARELESSNESS as RESPONSE is to** (A) answer; (B) stimulus; (C) correct; (D) effect; (E) good
1834. A	**1835. FULMINATION is to TRINITROTOLUENE as DISSIPATION is to** (A) tyranny; (B) gluttony; (C) concentration; (D) desire
1943. E	**1944. CAUCASIAN : SAXON : :** (A) white : colored; (B) Chinese : Indian; (C) furniture : chair; (D) carriage : horse; (E) city : house
2052. B	**2053. DERISIVE** (A) dividing; (B) furnishing; (C) reflecting; (D) laudatory; (E) suggesting
2161. C	**2162. Being ————, the child was not permitted to have his supper.** (A) refractory; (B) reticent; (C) vernal; (D) unctuous

81. E	**82. BONDAGE** (A) poverty; (B) redemption; (C) slavery; (D) retirement; (E) complaint
191. E	**192. ENTICE** (A) inform; (B) observe; (C) permit; (D) attract; (E) disobey
301. A	**302. MANDATORY** (A) insane; (B) obligatory; (C) evident; (D) strategic; (E) unequaled
411. C	**412. REVERIE** (A) abusive language; (B) love song; (C) backward step; (D) daydream; (E) holy man
521. C	**522. ADUMBRATION** (A) beginning; (B) error; (C) foreshadowing; (D) bruise
631. C	**632. BUMPTIOUS** (A) large; (B) self-assertive; (C) uneven; (D) clownish
741. D	**742. DIFFIDENT** (A) argumentative; (B) timid; (C) dissimilar; (D) discriminating
851. B	**852. FRENCH LEAVE** (A) special permission; (B) illegal entry; (C) hasty departure; (D) indefinite reprieve
961. C	**962. KUDOS** (A) African antelope; (B) Japanese wrestling; (C) fermented beverage; (D) renown
1071. C	**1072. PARLOUS** (A) loquacious; (B) debatable; (C) merry; (D) shocking

1181. C	**1182. ROTE** (A) indited; (B) alternating; (C) routine; (D) spiral
1290. D	**1291. VIS-A-VIS** (A) passport; (B) disguise; (C) insight; (D) opposite
1399. A	**1400. DELFT** (A) pottery; (B) cave; (C) alluvial deposit; (D) crystalline larkspur
1508. C	**1509. LAMPOON** (A) squib; (B) eel; (C) buoy; (D) candelabra
1617. B	**1618. RACHITIC** (A) racy; (B) regal; (C) rosy; (D) rickety
1726. B	**1727. CANVAS is to PAINT as CLAY is to** (A) mold; (B) cloth; (C) statue; (D) art; (E) aesthetic
1835. B	**1836. EDIFICATION is to AWARENESS as EXACERBATION is to** (A) soreness; (B) excitement; (C) reduction; (D) deliberation
1944. C	**1945. OCTAVO : BINDING : :** (A) pica : printing; (B) music : octave; (C) day : week; (D) pamphlet : book; (E) ruler : artist
2053. D	**2054. DEBILITATE** (A) encourage; (B) insinuate; (C) prepare; (D) turn away; (E) strengthen
2162. A *Page* 164	**2163. The chairman's ————— speech swayed the audience to favor his proposal.** (A) cursory; (B) blatant; (C) ancillary; (D) cogent

82. **C**	**83. BOUNTEOUS** (A) insidious; (B) obligated; (C) generous; (D) buxom
192. **D**	**193. EPICURE** (A) gourmet; (B) analysis; (C) historic poem; (D) remedy
302. **B**	**303. MAUDLIN** (A) humorous; (B) weakly sentimental; (C) pictorial; (D) oddly shaped; (E) closely related
412. **D**	**413. REVOCATION** (A) certificate; (B) repeal; (C) animation; (D) license; (E) plea
522. **C**	**523. ADVENTITIOUS** (A) risky; (B) counterfeit; (C) inventive; (D) accidental
632. **B**	**633. BURGEE** (A) nautical flag; (B) colorful antipodean bird; (C) hot, parching wind; (D) coarse sacking cloth
742. **B**	**743. DILETTANTE** (A) pickle; (B) dabbler; (C) relative; (D) spread
852. **C**	**853. FRIABLE** (A) easily frightened; (B) capable of producing young; (C) cookable; (D) easily crumbled
962. **D**	**963. LACHRYMOSE** (A) fearful; (B) tearful; (C) fretful; (D) porous
1072. **D**	**1073. PARSIMONY** (A) indulgence; (B) lavishness; (C) frivolity; (D) frugality

1182. C	**1183. SACROSANCT** (A) sacerdotal; (B) sanctimonious; (C) sacramental; (D) sacred
1291. D	**1292. VITIATE** (A) enliven; (B) create; (C) impair; (D) defame
1400. A	**1401. DÉMARCHE** (A) misprision; (B) downfall; (C) course of action; (D) bad bargain
1509. A	**1510. LAPIDATED** (A) set with precious stones; (B) petrified; (C) covered with thin fur; (D) stoned to death
1618. D	**1619. RADDLED** (A) punctured; (B) meretricious; (C) zealous; (D) rouged
1727. A	**1728. FISH is to FIN as BIRD is to** (A) wing; (B) five; (C) feet; (D) beak; (E) feathers
1836. A	**1837. GASTRONOMICAL is to GOURMET as GEOLOGICAL is to** (A) raconteur; (B) entomologist; (C) etymologist; (D) paleontologist
1945. A	**1946. CLASSIC : GREECE : :** (A) Empire : France; (B) Roman : Italy; (C) colonialism : India; (D) Ionic : Rome; (E) new : America
2054. E	**2055. OPULENT** (A) fearful; (B) free; (C) oversized; (D) trustful; (E) impoverished
2163. D	**2164. He is quite ————— and, therefore, easily —————.** (A) callow - deceived; (B) lethal - perceived; (C) fetal - conceived; (D) limpid - received

83. C	84. BOUNTY (A) limit; (B) boastfulness; (C) cheerfulness; (D) reward; (E) punishment
193. A	194. EPITAPH (A) witty saying; (B) satirical poem; (C) concluding speech; (D) seat beside a wall; (E) inscription on a tomb
303. B	304. MEAGER (A) excessive; (B) harmonious; (C) fearful; (D) commonplace; (E) scanty
413. B	414. RIGOR (A) activity; (B) shagginess; (C) sorrow; (D) severity; (E) repayment
523. D	524. AFFABLE (A) courteous; (B) diseased; (C) obligated; (D) influential
633. A	634. BURGEON (A) sprout; (B) burden; (C) batter; (D) goad
743. B	744. DISCOMFITED (A) pained; (B) balked; (C) ridiculed; (D) exhausted
853. D	854. FULIGINOUS (A) overflowing; (B) luminous; (C) smoky; (D) angry
963. B	964. LACONIC (A) commonplace; (B) stoical; (C) concise; (D) flamboyant
1073. D	1074. PARTHIAN SHAFT (A) last retort; (B) adjunct to a Persian chariot; (C) ancient Near-Eastern tunnel; (D) vigorous onslaught

1183. D	**1184. SALINE** (A) salty; (B) dirty; (C) pallid; (D) conspicuous
1292. C	**1293. VOTARY** (A) enthusiast; (B) poller; (C) atheist; (D) official
1401. C	**1402. DEMESNE** (A) domain; (B) bearing; (C) debasement; (D) slander
1510. D	**1511. LARES** (A) spinning fates; (B) household deities; (C) animal dens; (D) part of the windpipe
1619. D	**1620. RAGTAG** (A) flower; (B) barbecue; (C) game; (D) mob
1728. A	**1729. INCH is to SQUARE INCH as SQUARE INCH is to** (A) inch; (B) cubic inch; (C) foot; (D) yard; (E) cube
1837. D	**1838. ECCLESIASTICAL is to CHURCH as CULINARY is to** (A) bedroom; (B) closet; (C) knife; (D) kitchen
1946. A	**1947. MARACAS : DANCER : :** (A) xylophone : player; (B) metronome : pianist; (C) tambourine : gypsy; (D) sample : salesman; (E) wrench : plumber
2055. E	**2056. BLANDISHMENT** (A) brunette; (B) criticism; (C) ostentation; (D) praise; (E) return
2164. A	**2165. That ———— seems so out of place with those lovely little girls.** (A) shard; (B) hoyden; (C) tyro; (D) vanguard

84. **D**	**85. BULWARK** (A) target; (B) grass; (C) safeguard; (D) tail; (E) compartment
194. **E**	**195. EQUITABLE** (A) unbiased; (B) unjust; (C) unreasonable; (D) unfair
304. **E**	**305. MEANDERING** (A) cruel; (B) adjusting; (C) winding; (D) smooth; (E) combining
414. **D**	**415. RUDIMENTARY** (A) web-like; (B) elementary; (C) systematic; (D) structural; (E) discourteous
524. **A**	**525. AFFLATUS** (A) percussion; (B) inspiration; (C) amplification; (D) affectation
634. **A**	**635. BUTTRESS** (A) prop; (B) entice; (C) attack; (D) demolish
744. **B**	**745. DISCREET** (A) careless; (B) prudent; (C) truthful; (D) separate
854. **C**	**855. FULMINATE** (A) denounce; (B) flay; (C) dazzle; (D) smoke
964. **C**	**965. LACUNA** (A) gap; (B) layer; (C) satellite; (D) terseness
1074. **A**	**1075. PARVENU** (A) passerby; (B) apparition; (C) judicial district; (D) upstart

1184. A	1185. SANGUINE (A) hopeful; (B) murderous; (C) despairing; (D) ridden with guilt
1293. A	1294. VOUCHSAFE (A) escort; (B) acknowledge openly; (C) grant; (D) attest the truth of
1402. A	1403. DEMOTIC (A) mobile; (B) tyrannical; (C) popular; (D) fiendish
1511. B	1512. LAUDANUM (A) a pendant ornate with gems; (B) crown of laurel; (C) ascription or hymn of praise; (D) tincture of opium
1620. D	1621. RAMOSE (A) plethoric; (B) tearful; (C) branching; (D) sorrowful
1729. B	1730. SOLUTION is to MYSTERY as LEARNING is to (A) study; (B) comics; (C) college; (D) school; (E) detective
1838. D	1839. DICHOTOMY is to DIVISION as DISSEMBLE is to (A) feign; (B) assemble; (C) resemble; (D) return
1947. B	1948. BOTTLE : ALCOHOLISM : : (A) pill : dope; (B) tranquilizer : emotions; (C) atomizer : sinusitis; (D) candy : overweight; (E) perfume : smell
2056. B	2057. CRYPTIC (A) appealing; (B) arched; (C) deathly; (D) revealing; (E) intricate
2165. B Page 170	2166. The sculptor will convert this ———— piece of clay into a beautiful bust. (A) virulent; (B) amorphous; (C) taciturn; (D) salient

85. C	**86. BUOYANT** (A) unwise; (B) cheerful; (C) alarming; (D) uncertain; (E) juvenile
195. A	**196. EVASIVE** (A) penetrating; (B) blotting; (C) shifty; (D) broad; (E) unsympathetic
305. C	**306. MEDITATE** (A) rest; (B) stare; (C) doze; (D) make peace; (E) reflect
415. B	**416. SACRILEGE** (A) desecration; (B) sacrifice; (C) vestry; (D) sexton
525. B	**526. AKIMBO** (A) hand on hip and elbow turned out; (B) without direction of any kind; (C) astride; (D) askew
635. A	**636. CACHE** (A) acquire; (B) hold; (C) collect; (D) hide
745. B	**746. DISCRETE** (A) not orderly; (B) subtle; (C) circumspect; (D) distinct
855. A	**856. FURBISH** (A) provide; (B) burnish; (C) deck with ruffles; (D) incite
965. A	**966. LAISSEZ-FAIRE** (A) without interference; (B) lacking competence; (C) with consideration; (D) under inspection
1075. D	**1076. PATOIS** (A) inner court; (B) perfume; (C) sympathetic sorrow; (D) provincial speech

1185. A	**1186. SAPID** (A) tasty; (B) wise; (C) insipid; (D) stupid
1294. C	**1295. WAG** (A) humorous fellow; (B) talebearer; (C) profligate; (D) chatterbox
1403. C	**1404. DENOUEMENT** (A) exordium; (B) diabolism; (C) solution; (D) climax
1512. D	**1513. LEMAN** (A) mistress; (B) citrus fruit; (C) houseboy; (D) rodent
1621. C	**1622. RATIOCINATION** (A) ecstasy; (B) zeal; (C) reasoning; (D) proportion
1730. A	**1731. PARIAH is to OUTCAST as MULLAH is to** (A) mourner; (B) judge; (C) martinet; (D) constable; (E) parish
1839. A	**1840. CREPUSCULAR is to INDISTINCT as CURSORY is to** (A) profane; (B) egregious; (C) superficial; (D) unique
1948. D	**1949. MACE : MAJESTY : :** (A) queen : king; (B) sword : soldier; (C) diploma : knowledge; (D) book : story; (E) house : security
2057. D	**2058. RAUCOUS** (A) euphonious; (B) loud; (C) querulous; (D) rational; (E) violent
2166. B	**2167. His ———— had no place in our serious conversation.** (A) badinage; (B) viscosity; (C) concatenation; (D) valence

86. B	87. CANDOR (A) sociability; (B) outspokenness; (C) grief; (D) light; (E) flattery
196. C	197. EXCERPT (A) omission; (B) sales tax; (C) cancellation; (D) pleasure trip; (E) selected passage
306. E	307. MERGER (A) leniency; (B) plunge; (C) detective; (D) magician; (E) consolidation
416. A	417. SAGE (A) wise man; (B) halo; (C) gold salt; (D) ear
526. A	527. ALFRESCO (A) fresh food; (B) spring flood; (C) water color; (D) in the open air
636. D	637. CACHET (A) hidden compartment; (B) intrigue; (C) distinctive quality; (D) esteem
746. D	747. DISINTERESTED (A) opposed; (B) contemptuous; (C) superficial; (D) impartial
856. B	857. FURTIVE (A) uncertain; (B) careful; (C) indirect; (D) sly
966. A	967. LASSITUDE (A) leather rope; (B) beauty; (C) permanency; (D) weariness
1076. D	1077. PAUCITY (A) emaciation; (B) dearth; (C) shrinkage; (D) severity

1186. **A**	**1187. SARDONIC** (A) like a gem; (B) derisive; (C) fleshy; (D) descriptive
1295. **A**	**1296. WATERSHED** (A) artificial passage for water; (B) sudden copious rainfall; (C) drainage area; (D) line marking ebb or flow of tide
1404. **C**	**1405. DERACINATED** (A) unmanned; (B) deprived of citizenship; (C) uprooted; (D) devalued
1513. **A**	**1514. LENITIVE** (A) acrimonious; (B) emollient; (C) painful; (D) elongating
1622. **C**	**1623. REBECK** (A) percussion instrument; (B) recall; (C) recorder; (D) stringed musical instrument
1731. **B**	**1732. PLETHORIC is to SUPERFLUOUS as** **SUBLIMINAL is to** (A) subterranean; (B) subconscious; (C) superb; (D) fantastic; (E) advertised
1840. **C**	**1841. VIXEN is to SEAMSTRESS as BACCHUS** **is to** (A) Ceres; (B) Neptune; (C) Venus; (D) Minerva
1949. **C**	**1950. ARTIST : TALENT : :** (A) doctor : sickness; (B) chief : boss; (C) machinist : product; (D) policeman : government; (E) auditor : accuracy
2058. **A**	**2059. AVIDITY** (A) friendliness; (B) generosity; (C) resentment; (D) speed; (E) thirst
2167. **A**	**2168. Her ————— manner embarrassed the** **others at the party.** (A) affable; (B) tractable; (C) sapid; (D) gauche

87. **B**	**88. CAPRICE** (A) wisdom; (B) ornament; (C) pillar; (D) whim; (E) energy
197. **E**	**198. EXONERATE** (A) free from blame; (B) warn; (C) drive out; (D) overcharge; (E) plead
307. **E**	**308. METAPHOR** (A) unrhymed poetry; (B) change of structure; (C) part of a foot; (D) implied comparison; (E) signal light
417. **A**	**418. SAGACITY** (A) ferocity; (B) generosity; (C) wisdom; (D) daring
527. **D**	**528. ALLEGORY** (A) concluding speech; (B) collection of epigrams; (C) symbolic story; (D) commendatory inscription
637. **C**	**638. CADENZA** (A) dance; (B) solo passage; (C) cabinet; (D) rise in volume
747. **D**	**748. DISQUISITION** (A) colloquy; (B) essay; (C) dialogue; (D) torture
857. **D**	**858. FULSOME** (A) sincere; (B) replete; (C) complete; (D) disgusting
967. **D**	**968. LAUGH IN ONE'S SLEEVE** (A) be humiliated; (B) chuckle slyly; (C) exult; (D) have the laugh turned against one
1077. **B**	**1078. PECCADILLO** (A) social blunder; (B) carnivorous animal; (C) minor fault; (D) small-sized cigar

1187. B	**1188. SATIETY** (A) excess; (B) inclination to evil; (C) common bond; (D) figure of speech
1296. C	**1297. WEALD** (A) happiness; (B) plain; (C) sky; (D) affliction
1405. C	**1406. DESCANT** (A) comment freely; (B) adjudicate fairly; (C) authorize; (D) disparage
1514. B	**1515. LIGATURE** (A) drug store; (B) bandage; (C) tendril; (D) lawsuit
1623. D	**1624. RECIDIVISM** (A) relapse into criminal habits; (B) addiction; (C) rule by the proletariat; (D) solvency
1732. B	**1733. ALUMNUS is to ALUMNA as PRINCE is to** (A) castle; (B) king; (C) knight; (D) country; (E) princess
1841. B	**1842. GLABROUS is to HIRSUTE as FACTITIOUS is to** (A) authentic; (B) fictional; (C) fluent; (D) replete
1950. E	**1951. PEDAGOGUE : LEARNING : :** (A) teaching : books; (B) professor : erudition; (C) Plato : pedant; (D) schoolmaster : ABC's; (E) books : knowledge
2059. B	**2060. HIATUS** (A) branch; (B) disease; (C) gaiety; (D) insect; (E) closing
2168. D	**2169. In a state of ————, we are likely to have ————.** (A) ochlocracy - havoc; (B) bureaucracy - respect; (C) theocracy - sin; (D) desuetude - activity

88. D	**89. CARDIAC** (A) mental; (B) circulatory; (C) heart; (D) tender; (E) crimson
198. A	**199. EXPEDITE** (A) hinder; (B) harm; (C) send; (D) hasten
308. D	**309. MOBILE** (A) changeable; (B) scornful; (C) mechanical; (D) stylish; (E) solid
418. C	**419. SALLOW** (A) yellowish; (B) external; (C) healing; (D) quiet; (E) vague
528. C	**529. ALLEVIATE** (A) aggravate; (B) augment; (C) mitigate; (D) amuse
638. B	**639. CADRE** (A) sponge; (B) rhythm; (C) framework; (D) bounder
748. B	**749. DISSEMBLE** (A) feign; (B) take apart; (C) undress; (D) sow seeds
858. D	**859. GARISH** (A) naive; (B) polished; (C) showy; (D) rusty
968. B	**969. LAVE** (A) dislike; (B) heat; (C) wash; (D) defeat
1078. C	**1079. PECULATOR** (A) gambler; (B) herdsman; (C) embezzler; (D) officer

1188. A	**1189. SATRAP** (A) subordinate ruler; (B) male woodland deity; (C) form of basalt rock; (D) device for entangling small game
1297. B	**1298. WELKIN** (A) sky; (B) countryside; (C) fire gong; (D) church bells
1406. A	**1407. DIDOES** (A) parts of wall surface; (B) antics; (C) heraldic devices; (D) vampires
1515. B	**1516. LIMN** (A) trim; (B) sprinkle; (C) conjure; (D) delineate
1624. A	**1625. RECUSANT** (A) recriminatory; (B) accusative; (C) non-conformist; (D) recuperative
1733. E	**1734. GANDER is to GOOSE as BULL is to** (A) cow; (B) hog; (C) pig; (D) lamb; (E) reap
1842. A	**1843. CHOLERIC is to PLACID as BANAL is to** (A) portly; (B) flippant; (C) reasonable; (D) unique
1951. D	**1952. STICK : DISCIPLINE : :** (A) bat : ball; (B) carrot : incentive; (C) hit : hurt; (D) book : learning; (E) seat : rest
2060. E	**2061. PLENARY** (A) easy; (B) stolid; (C) incomplete; (D) rewarding; (E) untrustworthy
2169. A	**2170. Knowledge cannot thrive where there is** ————. (A) parturition; (B) nescience; (C) protocol; (D) neoclassicism

| 89. | 90. CARDINAL |
| C | (A) independent; (B) well-organized; (C) subordinate; (D) dignified; (E) chief |

| 199. | 200. EXPLOIT |
| D | (A) declaration; (B) deed; (C) ambition; (D) outrage; (E) conspiracy |

| 309. | 310. MOLLIFY |
| A | (A) change; (B) soften; (C) discolor; (D) inure |

| 419. | 420. SAVOR |
| A | (A) salvage; (B) exception; (C) taste; (D) scab |

| 529. | 530. ALLOTROPIC |
| C | (A) duly apportioned; (B) related to a system of medical practice; (C) located close to the Tropic of Cancer; (D) existing in two or more forms |

| 639. | 640. CAESURA |
| C | (A) imperial lineage; (B) type of operation; (C) division of time; (D) break in rhythm of verse |

| 749. | 750. DISSIMULATE |
| A | (A) differ; (B) spread; (C) cheat; (D) feign |

| 859. | 860. GARROTE |
| C | (A) vegetate; (B) strangle; (C) repeat; (D) dance |

| 969. | 970. LECTERN |
| C | (A) triptych; (B) reading desk in a church; (C) lamp; (D) proscenium arch |

| 1079. | 1080. PECUNIARY |
| C | (A) miserly; (B) monetary; (C) unusual; (D) small |

1189. A	**1190. SATURNINE** (A) gloomy; (B) rotund; (C) ancient; (D) satisfying
1298. A	**1299. WELTER** (A) ridge; (B) turmoil; (C) vault of heaven; (D) conglomeration
1407. B	**1408. DINT** (A) method; (B) grime; (C) stroke; (D) noise; (E) care
1516. D	**1517. LITIGIOUS** (A) sacramental; (B) disputatious; (C) stony; (D) obnoxious
1625. C	**1626. REDACT** (A) mark; (B) edit; (C) repeat; (D) revive
1734. A	**1735. BLANCHED is to PALLOR as TELIC is to** (A) form; (B) sum; (C) purpose; (D) beginning; (E) cataract
1843. D	**1844. CADENZA is to MUSIC as LOB is to** (A) baseball; (B) football; (C) cricket; (D) boxing
1952. B	**1953. RETREAT : DEFEAT : :** (A) advance : capitulate; (B) march : forward; (C) surround : surrender; (D) retire : battle; (E) retrench : bankruptcy
2061. C	**2062. CAPRICIOUS** (A) active; (B) stable; (C) opposed; (D) sheeplike; (E) slippery
2170. B	**2171. ———— is a phase of the study of penology.** (A) recidivism; (B) electicism; (C) hematosis; (D) hydrometry

90. E	**91. CARICATURE** (A) famine; (B) exaggeration; (C) list; (D) consideration; (E) expense
200. B	**201. EXPUNGE** (A) efface; (B) amplify; (C) soften; (D) jostle
310. B	**311. MONOMIAL** (A) eyeglass; (B) soliloquy; (C) one term; (D) one tone
420. C	**421. SCRIMP** (A) dissipate; (B) save; (C) waste; (D) lavish
530. D	**531. ALLUSION** (A) conspiracy; (B) deposit; (C) reference; (D) condition
640. D	**641. CAISSON** (A) capital letter; (B) structure in which men can work on river bottoms; (C) ideograph; (D) type of cheese
750. D	**751. DISTAFF SIDE** (A) left side; (B) right side; (C) proper side to mount a horse; (D) female side
860. B	**861. GASTRONOMY** (A) classification of mollusks; (B) science of the care of the stomach; (C) gas diffusion; (D) art of good eating
970. B	**971. LEGERDEMAIN** (A) law of succession; (B) medieval manuscript; (C) legalized seizure; (D) sleight of hand
1080. B	**1081. PELLUCID** (A) radiant; (B) limpid; (C) discerning; (D) trimmed with fur

1190. A	**1191. SCANTLING** (A) small amount; (B) scathing irony; (C) young animal; (D) piece of armor
1299. B	**1300. WHEREFORE** (A) whilom; (B) why; (C) whence; (D) whither
1408. C	**1409. DIPSOMANIA** (A) fear of water; (B) irresistible craving for drink; (C) urge for power; (D) tendency to gamble
1517. B	**1518. LITOTES** (A) hyperbole; (B) oxymoron; (C) synecdoche; (D) understatement
1626. B	**1627. REDACTION** (A) recoil; (B) propaganda; (C) movement of a rifle; (D) new edition
1735. C	**1736. SYSTOLE is to DIASTOLE as TRUNCATION is to** (A) shortening; (B) shrinkage; (C) elongation; (D) mutilation; (E) trunk
1844. C	**1845. ARROGATE is to USURP as CLOY is to** (A) collect; (B) employ; (C) glut; (D) cut
1953. E	**1954. RUN : RAILROAD : :** (A) walk : pogo stick; (B) swim : boat; (C) fly : airline; (D) sink : bottle; (E) horn : automobile
2062. B	**2063. SPECIOUS** (A) scanty; (B) particular; (C) genuine; (D) suspicious; (E) vigorous
2171. A	**2172. The ———— of war is death and cruelty.** (A) sirocco; (B) rutabaga; (C) beldam; (D) quiddity

91. B	**92. CARIES** (A) canaries; (B) cracks; (C) decay; (D) trills
201. A	**202. EXTERMINATE** (A) annihilate; (B) asphyxiate; (C) finish; (D) decline
311. C	**312. MUNDANE** (A) spiritual; (B) sophisticated; (C) lasting; (D) worldly
421. B	**422. SCRUTINIZE** (A) examine closely; (B) praise openly; (C) drink; (D) tighten; (E) write freely
531. C	**532. ALTER EGO** (A) business partner; (B) striking personality; (C) bosom friend; (D) guide
641. B	**642. CAJOLE** (A) promise; (B) coax; (C) reason; (D) deter
751. D	**752. DISTRAIT** (A) crooked; (B) narrow; (C) broken; (D) absent-minded
861. D	**862. GAUD** (A) epithet; (B) trinket; (C) spur; (D) taunt
971. D	**972. LEES** (A) scuppers awash; (B) dregs; (C) onions; (D) meadows
1081. B	**1082. PENSIVE** (A) sorrowful; (B) dreamy; (C) dependent; (D) doubtful

1191. A	1192. SCOTCH (A) stamp out; (B) burn; (C) scourge; (D) spread
1300. B	1301. WHITE ELEPHANT (A) valuable gift; (B) troublesome possession; (C) faithful servant; (D) retentive memory
1409. B	1410. DIRL (A) dread; (B) vibrate; (C) foil; (D) lament; (E) disperse
1518. D	1519. LOGGIA (A) gallery; (B) sofa; (C) cabin; (D) villa
1627. D	1628. REPINE (A) complain; (B) lie down; (C) snatch; (D) brood
1736. C	1737. TALKING is to YELLING as DANCING is to (A) rejoicing; (B) mixing; (C) prancing; (D) singing; (E) slinging
1845. C	1846. DENIGRATE is to DEFAMER as MEDIATE is to (A) mathematician; (B) arbitrator; (C) employer; (D) laborer
1954. C	1955. ELIXIR : PILL : : (A) life : health; (B) water : ice; (C) bottle : box; (D) mystery : story; (E) nurse : doctor
2063. C	2064. EXTIRPATE (A) besmirch; (B) clean; (C) renew; (D) favor; (E) subdivide
2172. D	2173. The conceited soldier was forward and ———— in his attitude. (A) mundane; (B) thrasonical; (C) gratuitous; (D) laconic

92. C	**93. CAUCUS** (A) dispersal; (B) corpse; (C) meeting; (D) cosmetic
202. A	**203. EXUDE** (A) accuse; (B) discharge; (C) inflect; (D) appropriate; (E) distress
312. D	**313. NEFARIOUS** (A) wicked; (B) holy; (C) needy; (D) greedy
422. A	**423. SCRUTINY** (A) muscle; (B) advertising; (C) scowl; (D) close examination; (E) tense situation
532. C	**533. AMANUENSIS** (A) jehu; (B) messenger; (C) secretary; (D) soldier
642. B	**643. CALCAREOUS** (A) corpse-like; (B) heat-producing; (C) chalky; (D) gourd-shaped
752. D	**753. DIURNAL** (A) official; (B) routine; (C) medicinal; (D) daily
862. B	**863. GENRE** (A) aristocracy; (B) style; (C) environment; (D) birthmark
972. B	**973. LEONINE** (A) tortuous; (B) celebrating; (C) drawn out; (D) lion-like
1082. B	**1083. PENURIOUS** (A) miserly; (B) studious; (C) bankrupt; (D) notorious

1192. A	**1193. SCRUPULOUS** (A) upright; (B) exact; (C) neat and clean; (D) dishonest
1301. B	**1302. WINDLASS** (A) conclusion; (B) machine; (C) legacy; (D) shroud
1410. B	**1411. DISSIDENCE** (A) efflorescence; (B) propinquity; (C) dubiety; (D) disagreement
1519. A	**1520. LUBRICOUS** (A) mercenary; (B) smooth; (C) tubular; (D) thrifty
1628. A	**1629. REPLICATION** (A) echo; (B) repeat mechanism; (C) analysis; (D) erosion
1737. C	**1738. REVERT is to REVERSION as SYMPATHIZE is to** (A) sympathic; (B) symposium; (C) sympathy; (D) sympathizer; (E) simplicity
1846. B	**1847. INCHOATE is to TERMINAL as SATURNINE is to** (A) mercurial; (B) planetary; (C) saturated; (D) relaxed
1955. D	**1956. SUNDER is to CONSOLIDATE as TANGIBLE is to** (A) abstract; (B) tasty; (C) possible; (D) tangled
2064. C	**2065. EQUIVOCAL** (A) positive; (B) medium; (C) monotonous; (D) musical; (E) well-balanced
2173. B	**2174. Being a man of maxims, he was ———— in what he said.** (A) sententious; (B) transmogrified; (C) sebaceous; (D) sentient

93. C	**94. CHAGRIN** (A) delight; (B) alter; (C) wreck; (D) dismay
203. B	**204. EXULTANT** (A) essential; (B) elated; (C) praiseworthy; (D) plentiful; (E) high-priced
313. A	**314. NEUTRALIZE** (A) entangle; (B) strengthen; (C) counteract; (D) combat; (E) converse
423. D	**424. SEETHE** (A) roast; (B) tool; (C) boil; (D) smoke
533. C	**534. AMBIVALENCE** (A) simultaneous attraction and repulsion; (B) ability to walk; (C) duality; (D) equal adeptness with right hand and left hand
643. C	**644. CALLIGRAPHY** (A) elegant writing; (B) map making; (C) telegraph memorandum; (D) terminology of ceramics
753. D	**754. DIVULGE** (A) publish; (B) separate; (C) amuse; (D) deprive
863. B	**864. GERIATRICS** (A) science of old age and its diseases; (B) study of germs; (C) shoddy building practices; (D) low form of comedy
973. D	**974. LÈSE MAJESTÉ** (A) divine right of kings; (B) crime against the king; (C) royal property; (D) royal bearing
1083. A	**1084. PENURY** (A) shadow; (B) poverty; (C) legality; (D) contest

1193. B	**1194. SCURF** (A) rough water; (B) menial attendant; (C) coarse linen; (D) dandruff
1302. B	**1303. WIZENED** (A) witless; (B) shriveled; (C) wiry; (D) stooped
1411. D	**1412. DIVAGATION** (A) primary formulation; (B) digression; (C) equitable apportionment; (D) subterranean tunnel
1520. B	**1521. LUCUBRATE** (A) illuminate brilliantly; (B) lament unduly; (C) work or study laboriously; (D) deprecate unceasingly
1629. A	**1630. RETICULATE** (A) embellished; (B) netlike; (C) required; (D) subservient
1738. C	**1739. REGRESSIVE is to REGRESS as STERILE is to** (A) sterilization; (B) sterilize; (C) sterility; (D) sterilizer; (E) storage
1847. A	**1848. LITTORAL is to COAST as PECTORAL is to** (A) throat; (B) leg; (C) skeleton; (D) chest
1956. A	**1957. DEVIOUS is to CIRCUITOUS as YIELDING is to** (A) yodeling; (B) wielding; (C) simmering; (D) submissive
2065. A	**2066. BENISON** (A) approval; (B) curse; (C) gift; (D) prayer; (E) reward
2174. A	**2175. His ————— remarks are too stupid to be taken —————.** (A) empyreal - lightly; (B) puerperal - slowly; (C) lacunal - violently; (D) vapid - seriously

94. D	**95. CHARD** (A) chore; (B) scorched; (C) beet; (D) game
204. B	**205. FACILE** (A) extraordinary; (B) queer; (C) breakable; (D) easy; (E) impossible
314. C	**315. NOCTURNAL** (A) musical; (B) of the night; (C) owl-like; (D) pertaining to illness; (E) romantic
424. C	**425. SEGREGATE** (A) multiply; (B) encircle; (C) conform; (D) isolate; (E) deny
534. A	**535. AMELIORATE** (A) harden; (B) coarsen; (C) aggravate; (D) improve
644. A	**645. CALUMNIOUS** (A) disastrous; (B) conspiratorial; (C) querulous; (D) slanderous
754. A	**755. DOCTRINAL** (A) pragmatic; (B) abstruse; (C) dogmatic; (D) orthodox
864. A	**865. GERMANE** (A) relevant; (B) obsolete; (C) pallid; (D) susceptible
974. B	**975. LETHAL** (A) spirited; (B) cooling; (C) fatal; (D) highly charged
1084. B	**1085. PERADVENTURE** (A) by accident; (B) in danger; (C) under oath; (D) through courage

1194. D	1195. SEDENTARY (A) stationary; (B) migratory; (C) rudimentary; (D) obsolescent
1303. B	1304. WRAITH (A) anger; (B) perversity; (C) calamity; (D) apparition
1412. B	1413. DOT (A) fool; (B) fabric; (C) crack; (D) dowry
1521. C	1522. LUSTRUM (A) an illustrated pamphlet; (B) a lusty person; (C) a seven-day period; (D) a five-year period
1630. B	1631. RETROUSSÉ (A) with a wide hem; (B) turned up; (C) trimmed with lace; (D) turned down
1739. B	1740. DOWN is to DOWNY as AGE is to (A) period; (B) old; (C) ancient; (D) historic; (E) stagnant
1848. D	1849. BUCOLIC is to PEACEFUL as CIMMERIAN is to (A) warlike; (B) tenebrous; (C) doubtful; (D) smirking
1957. D	1958. SATURNINE is to JOCOSE as OPULENCE is to (A) pollution; (B) gem; (C) opera; (D) penury
2066. B	2067. SANGUINE (A) limp; (B) mechanical; (C) muddy; (D) livid; (E) stealthy
2175. D	2176. The ———— was very informative during the trip. (A) censer; (B) centaur; (C) cicerone; (D) burgeon

95. C	**96. CHASTENED** (A) construed; (B) pursued; (C) hurt; (D) refined
205. D	**206. FACTION** (A) clique; (B) judgment; (C) truth; (D) type of architecture; (E) health
315. B	**316. NOMENCLATURE** (A) election; (B) system of names; (C) morality; (D) grammar; (E) migration
425. D	**426. SERRATED** (A) dehydrated; (B) stretched; (C) sawtoothed; (D) intensified
535. D	**536. AMENABLE** (A) tractable; (B) depressing; (C) neighborly; (D) kind
645. D	**646. CALUMNY** (A) evil; (B) gossip; (C) ceremonial; (D) slander
755. C	**756. DOLT** (A) prankster; (B) stupid fellow; (C) manikin; (D) hobbledehoy
865. A	**866. GETHSEMANE** (A) herb; (B) sacred offering; (C) last judgment; (D) scene or occasion of suffering
975. C	**976. LEXICON** (A) Bible; (B) lawbook; (C) dictionary; (D) rostrum
1085. A	**1086. PEREGRINATE** (A) travel; (B) investigate; (C) find fault; (D) perceive with clarity

1195. A	**1196. SEDGE** (A) privet; (B) marsh grass; (C) selvage; (D) sage
1304. D	**1305. SYNONYMS** **Very difficult**
1413. D	**1414. DOXOLOGY** (A) right reasoning; (B) canon law; (C) papal bull; (D) hymn of praise to God
1522. D	**1523. MACADAM** (A) Australian shrub; (B) ring-tailed monkey; (C) heavy staff; (D) broken stone
1631. B	**1632. RODOMONTADE** (A) slice of meat rolled about a minced filling; (B) publicly posted lampoon; (C) vainglorious boasting; (D) whirling dance
1740. B	**1741. I is to MINE as MAN is to** (A) men; (B) his; (C) man's; (D) mine; (E) its
1849. B	**1850. LIMPID is to LUCID as TURBID is to** (A) torpid; (B) muddy; (C) truculent; (D) urban
1958. D	**1959. INTEMPERATE is to ABSTEMIOUS as** **SOMBER is to** (A) sleepy; (B) jaunty; (C) rhythmic; (D) soupy
2067. D	**2068. SURCEASE** (A) inception; (B) hope; (C) resignation; (D) sleep; (E) sweetness
2176. C	**2177. A ———— and the principle of monogamy** **are poles apart.** (A) seraglio; (B) purlieu; (C) shallop; (D) benison

96. D	**97. CHIMERICAL** (A) imaginary; (B) flimsy; (C) blazing; (D) smoking
206. A	**207. FEASIBLE** (A) indefinite; (B) practicable; (C) inadvisable; (D) edible; (E) prominent
316. B	**317. NONCHALANCE** (A) interest; (B) poverty; (C) care; (D) indifference
426. C	**427. SHACKLE** (A) oscillate; (B) enliven; (C) tremble; (D) hamper
536. A	**537. AMORPHOUS** (A) sleep-inducing; (B) powdered; (C) shapeless; (D) crystalline
646. D	**647. CALYX** (A) gelatinous substance; (B) helmet; (C) soft palate; (D) external part of a flower
756. B	**757. DORMANT** (A) agile; (B) inactive; (C) profound; (D) docile
866. D	**867. GIBBET** (A) globular vessel; (B) animal bone; (C) gallows; (D) senseless remark
976. C	**977. LICENTIOUS** (A) permissible; (B) licensed; (C) dissolute; (D) covetous
1086. A	**1087. PEREMPTORY** (A) dictatorial; (B) extemporaneous; (C) fervent; (D) prompt

1196. **B**	**1197. SEDULOUS** (A) roiled; (B) assiduous; (C) composed; (D) isolated
	1306. ABYSMAL (A) dire; (B) bottomless; (C) indigenous; (D) untold; (E) hounded
1414. **D**	**1415. DRAMSHOP** (A) pharmacy; (B) theatre; (C) barroom; (D) gossip
1523. **D**	**1524. MACERATE** (A) kill wantonly; (B) soften by soaking; (C) excise an internal organ; (D) intertwine strands
1632. **C**	**1633. RUBRIC** (A) rule of conduct; (B) plain song; (C) poem; (D) vespers
1741. **C**	**1742. DISLOYAL is to FAITHLESS as** **IMPERFECTION is to** (A) contamination; (B) depression; (C) foible; (D) decrepitude; (E) praise
1850. **B**	**1851. PHYSIOGNOMY is to FACE as** **NECROLOGY is to** (A) philosophy; (B) magic; (C) psychology; (D) mortality
1959. **B**	**1960. SCHOOL : TEACH : :** (A) book : cover; (B) wheel : tire; (C) knife : bread; (D) press : print; (E) teacher : learn
2068. **A**	**2069. SENTIENT** (A) emotional; (B) callous; (C) hostile; (D) sympathetic; (E) wise
2177. **A** *Page* 194	**2178. The mourning throng was preparing for a** ————. (A) wimple; (B) cirque; (C) riposte; (D) monody

97. **A**	**98. CHRONIC** (A) irritable; (B) historic; (C) sudden; (D) habitual; (E) timely
207. **B**	**208. FEMUR** (A) mare; (B) ape; (C) flower; (D) thigh bone
317. **D**	**318. NOVICE** (A) storyteller; (B) iceberg; (C) adolescent; (D) mythical creature; (E) beginner
427. **D**	**428. SHRIVEL** (A) creep; (B) cancel; (C) wither; (D) saturate
537. **C**	**538. AMULET** (A) small vase; (B) tribute; (C) talisman; (D) estuary
647. **D**	**648. CANAILLE** (A) lowest class of people; (B) dog hospital; (C) second estate; (D) French aristocracy
757. **B**	**758. DOTAGE** (A) senility; (B) dowry; (C) sofa; (D) hatred
867. **C**	**868. GLABROUS** (A) gaudy; (B) bald; (C) sharp; (D) shady
977. **C**	**978. LIMPID** (A) lucid; (B) flimsy; (C) unsteady; (D) watery
1087. **A**	**1088. PERFIDY** (A) fantastic purpose; (B) wantonness; (C) treachery; (D) aplomb

1197. **B**	**1198. SEMANTIC** (A) wordy; (B) oriental; (C) hypercritical; (D) pertaining to meaning
1306. **B**	**1307. ACCIDENCE** (A) gender; (B) foreign lexicon; (C) feminine rhyme; (D) grammatical inflection; (E) injuries
1415. **C**	**1416. DREE** (A) avoid; (B) endure; (C) force; (D) fritter; (E) drink
1524. **B**	**1525. MACULATED** (A) purified; (B) spotted; (C) pulverized; (D) serrated
1633. **A**	**1634. RUNE** (A) despoliation; (B) contumely; (C) alphabetical character; (D) luminous meteor
1742. **C**	**1743. MOHAIR is to GOAT as WOOL is to** (A) coat; (B) camel; (C) sheep; (D) horse; (E) chair
1851. **D**	**1852. ARCHAEOLOGIST is to ANTIQUITY as** **ICHTHYOLOGIST is to** (A) theology; (B) marine life; (C) horticulture; (D) mysticism
1960. **D**	**1961. POLITICIAN : STATESMAN : :** (A) fanatic : zealot; (B) lawyer : debate; (C) teacher : student; (D) journalist : novelist; (E) diplomat : United Nations
2069. **B**	**2070. OBVIATE** (A) grasp; (B) reform; (C) simplify; (D) smooth; (E) make necessary
2178. **D**	**2179. The will did not require witnesses, since** **it was ————.** (A) genocidic; (B) histrionic; (C) holographic; (D) ballistic

98. **D**	**99. CIRCUMVENT** (A) outwit; (B) get around; (C) open up; (D) cover
208. **D**	**209. FERRET** (A) agitate; (B) search out; (C) deny; (D) deliver; (E) rush forward
318. **E**	**319. OBESE** (A) lawful; (B) extremely fat; (C) challenging; (D) bowing deeply; (E) sad-faced
428. **C**	**429. SIGNIFICANT** (A) needless; (B) real; (C) childish; (D) important; (E) precise
538. **C**	**539. ANATHEMA** (A) curse; (B) blessing; (C) hymn; (D) benison
648. **A**	**649. CANARD** (A) rebus; (B) hoax; (C) scurrilous publication; (D) flattery
758. **A**	**759. DOUGHTY** (A) flabby and pale; (B) strong and valiant; (C) weak and craven; (D) crude and boorish
868. **B**	**869. GLUTINOUS** (A) sticky; (B) repulsively fat; (C) shimmering; (D) greedy
978. **A**	**979. LISSOM** (A) supple; (B) beautiful; (C) strong; (D) rippling
1088. **C**	**1089. PERFUNCTORY** (A) faithless; (B) mechanical; (C) perfect; (D) thorough

1198. D	**1199. SEND TO COVENTRY** (A) doom to destruction; (B) reduce in rank; (C) send on a fool's errand; (D) ostracize
1307. D	**1308. ACOLYTE** (A) rite; (B) attendant; (C) mystery; (D) celebrant
1416. B	**1417. DULCINEA** (A) organ stop; (B) deceiver; (C) sweetheart; (D) elderly woman
1525. B	**1526. MAGNUM** (A) vacuum tube; (B) century plant; (C) great artistic work; (D) two-quart bottle
1634. C	**1635. RUTABAGA** (A) alfalfa; (B) kind of corn; (C) turnip; (D) relish
1743. C	**1744. MASCULINE is to GENDER as RUBY is to** (A) dispute; (B) country; (C) color; (D) argument; (E) enemy
1852. B	**1853. ANNULAR is to RING as NUMMULAR is to** (A) limb; (B) sum; (C) shell; (D) coin
1961. A	**1962. CALIBRATOR : MEASURE : :** (A) plumber : wrench; (B) clamp : hold; (C) measure : tolerance; (D) ruler : line; (E) thermometer : temperature
2070. E	**2071. RANCOR** (A) dignity; (B) affection; (C) odor; (D) spite; (E) suspicion
2179. C	**2180. Man's fate is ———.** (A) ineluctable; (B) cerulean; (C) estivated; (D) spatulated

99. **B**	**100. CITE** (A) protest; (B) depart; (C) qucte; (D) agitate; (E) perform
209. **B**	**210. FERVOR** (A) artistic ability; (B) hatred; (C) kindness; (D) intense feeling; (E) coldness
319. **B**	**320. OBJECTIVE** (A) widespread; (B) witty; (C) sickly; (D) impersonal; (E) unpoetic
429. **D**	**430. SOBRIETY** (A) anger; (B) acting; (C) excess; (D) temperance
539. **A**	**540. ANDANTE** (A) moderately slow; (B) very fast; (C) sharp; (D) soft
649. **B**	**650. CAPITULATION** (A) sumptuous apparel; (B) beheading; (C) surrender; (D) bondage
759. **B**	**760. DOYEN** (A) chatelaine; (B) dowager; (C) seneschal; (D) dean
869. **A**	**870. GOUACHE** (A) water color; (B) engraving; (C) fresco; (D) etching
979. **A**	**980. LITTORAL** (A) ritualistic; (B) coastal; (C) belligerent; (D) unimaginative
1089. **B**	**1090. PERSIFLAGE** (A) farthingale; (B) song; (C) banter; (D) fruit

1199. D	1200. **SENESCENCE** (A) rebirth; (B) old age; (C) sleep walking; (D) bubbling over
1308. B	1309. **AFFLATUS** (A) conceit; (B) expansion; (C) inspiration; (D) debris
1417. C	1418. **DUNNAGE** (A) drayage; (B) lighterage; (C) baggage; (D) postage
1526. D	1527. **MAHATMA** (A) peace; (B) Indian prince; (C) high-minded; (D) a respectful form of address
1635. C	1636. **SACERDOTAL** (A) priestly; (B) sacrificial; (C) sugary; (D) profane
1744. C	1745. **SEED is to SOW as EGG is to** (A) pollinate; (B) hatch; (C) plant; (D) fruit; (E) earth
1853. D	1854. **DOWSER is to ROD as GEOMANCER is to** (A) stones; (B) maps; (C) plants; (D) configurations
1962. B	1963. **AUTHOR : NOVEL : :** (A) teacher : student; (B) reader : interest; (C) hero : win; (D) carpenter : cabinet; (E) doctor : cure
2071. B	2072. **DILATORY** (A) hairy; (B) happy-go-lucky; (C) ruined; (D) punctual; (E) well-to-do
2180. A	2181. How can you depend upon a person who is so ————? (A) protean; (B) somatic; (C) pensile; (D) empirical

100. C	**101. CLANDESTINE** (A) secret; (B) exclusive; (C) fortunate; (D) dated
210. D	**211. FICTITIOUS** (A) turbulent; (B) anxious; (C) assumed; (D) scanty
320. D	**321. OBLIVION** (A) hindrance; (B) accident; (C) courtesy; (D) forgetfulness; (E) old age
430. D	**431. SOMBER** (A) cutting; (B) colorful; (C) unusual; (D) melancholy; (E) jolly
540. A	**541. ANHYDROUS** (A) many-sided; (B) carefully divided; (C) many-headed; (D) destitute of water
650. C	**651. CAPRICIOUS** (A) unwavering; (B) wayward; (C) tortuous; (D) feeble
760. D	**761. DRAW THE LONGBOW** (A) prepare to fight; (B) make a supreme effort; (C) use a roundabout approach; (D) indulge in exaggeration
870. A	**871. GRANDILOQUENCE** (A) disguise; (B) banter; (C) pompousness; (D) loquacity
980. B	**981. LIVID** (A) gray-blue; (B) tense; (C) wrathful; (D) flushed
090. C	**1091. PERSPICACIOUS** (A) spiny; (B) lucid; (C) optical; (D) keen

1200. B	**1201. SENTENTIOUS** (A) opinionated; (B) sentimental; (C) pithy; (D) sensible
1309. C	**1310. AGNATE** (A) talismanic stone; (B) amulet; (C) related through males; (D) marble
1418. C	**1419. DYSTROPHY** (A) malnutrition; (B) dysuria; (C) atrophy; (D) leukemia
1527. C	**1528. MALMSEY** (A) sweet wine; (B) coarse fabric; (C) heavy-fleeced sheep; (D) cheap cutlery
1636. A	**1637. SALAD DAYS** (A) days of one's prime; (B) days of yore; (C) days of youthful inexperience; (D) halcyon days
1745. B	**1746. CONTEMPORARY is to PRESENT as POSTERITY is to** (A) past; (B) present; (C) modern; (D) ancient; (E) future
1854. D	**1855. ETYMOLOGY is to WORDS as HAGIOLOGY is to** (A) saints; (B) senility; (C) selling; (D) writing
1963. D	**1964. AMENDMENT : CONSTITUTION : :** (A) alien : consul; (B) emigrant : passport; (C) repair : machine; (D) immigrant : visa; (E) laborer : union
2072. D	**2073. EBULLITION** (A) bathing; (B) cooling; (C) refilling; (D) retiring; (E) returning
2181. A *Page* 202	**2182. A ————— would be interested in a ————— of that type.** (A) botanist - vignette; (B) soldier - maverick; (C) musician - caterwaul; (D) butcher - brioche

101. A	**102. CLICHÉ** (A) summary argument; (B) new information; (C) new hat; (D) trite phrase; (E) lock device
211. C	**212. FIDELITY** (A) selfishness; (B) faithfulness; (C) cruelty; (D) indifference; (E) weakness
321. D	**322. OBNOXIOUS** (A) dreamy; (B) visible; (C) angry; (D) daring; (E) objectionable
431. D	**432. SORCERY** (A) ancestry; (B) grief; (C) acidity; (D) filth; (E) witchcraft
541. D	**542. ANIMADVERSION** (A) vitality; (B) ire; (C) taboo; (D) stricture
651. B	**652. CAPRIOLE** (A) whim; (B) leap; (C) fern; (D) flourish
761. D	**762. DUDGEON** (A) resentment; (B) courage; (C) pride; (D) underground cell
871. D	**872. GRATUITOUS** (A) compensatory; (B) reciprocal; (C) incongruous; (D) superfluous
981. A	**982. LODESTAR** (A) guiding star; (B) vein of ore; (C) central star of constellation; (D) celestial body exercising magnetic force
1091. D	**1092. PERSPICACITY** (A) discernment; (B) secretion; (C) retention; (D) persuasiveness

1201. C	**1202. SENTIENT** (A) hostile; (B) sympathetic; (C) emotional; (D) capable of feeling
1310. C	**1311. AGGLUTINATION** (A) efflorescence; (B) adhesion; (C) acquisitiveness; (D) softening
1419. A	**1420. ECHINATED** (A) fossil-like; (B) isometric; (C) interspersed; (D) bristly
1528. A	**1529. MANDRAKE** (A) magician; (B) baboon; (C) bird; (D) herb
1637. C	**1638. SANHEDRIN** (A) fraternity; (B) public house; (C) assembly; (D) Indian officer; (E) regular polygon
1746. E	**1747. MOON is to EARTH as EARTH is to** (A) Mars; (B) moon; (C) sky; (D) sun; (E) orbit
1855. A	**1856. EUPEPTIC is to DIGESTION as EUPHEMISTIC is to** (A) speech; (B) race; (C) sound; (D) drug
1964. C	**1965. LAW : PROSECUTOR : :** (A) constitution : attorney general; (B) Congress : President; (C) legislation : governor; (D) Bible : minister; (E) athletics : boxer
2073. B	**2074. RELEGATE** (A) welcome; (B) deprive; (C) designate; (D) report; (E) request
2182. A	**2183. In India, a wealthy person may travel in a ———— borne by poles resting on men's shoulders.** (A) palanquin; (B) bibelot; (C) gambrel; (D) lampoon

102. **D**	**103. COALITION** (A) conference; (B) election; (C) union; (D) criticism; (E) fueling
212. **B**	**213. FLAIR** (A) aptitude; (B) bright light; (C) anger; (D) boasting remark; (E) frightening experience
322. **E**	**323. OBSCURITY** (A) slyness; (B) indistinctness; (C) ease; (D) disappearance; (E) sadness
432. **E**	**433. SPORADIC** (A) bad-tempered; (B) infrequent; (C) radical; (D) reckless; (E) humble
542. **D**	**543. ANODYNE** (A) machinelike; (B) soothing; (C) graceful; (D) nostalgic
652. **B**	**653. CAPSTAN** (A) quarter-deck of a ship; (B) anchor; (C) ship's funnel; (D) device for raising weights
762. **A**	**763. DUODECIMAL** (A) expressed in the scale of twelve; (B) type of ulcer; (C) a twentieth portion; (D) a musical dialogue
872. **D**	**873. GRIZZLED** (A) disheveled; (B) streaked with grey; (C) bristling; (D) fierce
982. **A**	**983. LUGUBRIOUS** (A) laborious; (B) healthful; (C) mournful; (D) bucolic
092. **A**	**1093. PERSPICUITY** (A) clarity; (B) persuasiveness; (C) thoroughness; (D) ambiguity

1202. D	1203. SEQUESTER (A) segregate; (B) follow; (C) accumulate; (D) organize
1311. B	1312. ALABASTER (A) translucent calcite; (B) detritus; (C) ruff; (D) antique ivory
1420. D	1421. ECOLOGICAL (A) tautological; (B) bucolic; (C) destructive; (D) environmental
1529. D	1530. MANDREL (A) spindle; (B) baboon; (C) jawbone; (D) lute
1638. C	1639. SARABAND (A) stately dance; (B) tiara-like ornament; (C) small lute; (D) insignia worn on left arm
1747. D	1748. ACUTE is to CHRONIC as INTENSE is to (A) sardonic; (B) tonic; (C) persistent; (D) pretty; (E) sick
1356. A	1857. LOGGIA is to GALLERY as JALOUSIE is to (A) lintel; (B) dowel; (C) jamb; (D) louver
1965. A	1966. PORT : SHIP : : (A) ship : storm; (B) ground : plane; (C) garage : automobile; (D) home : sailor; (E) safety : danger
2074. A	2075. RECONDITE (A) brittle; (B) exposed; (C) explored; (D) concealed; (E) uninformed
2183. A	2184. Suffering from ————, he decided to stay indoors. (A) claustrophobia; (B) agoraphobia; (C) chicanery; (D) patois

103. C	**104. COERCION** (A) force; (B) disgust; (C) suspicion; (D) pleasure; (E) criticism
213. A	**214. FLOUNDER** (A) investigate; (B) label; (C) struggle; (D) consent; (E) escape
323. B	**324. OMINOUS** (A) devouring everything; (B) all-inclusive; (C) having two meanings; (D) foreboding; (E) vegetable
433. B	**434. SQUALID** (A) unrealistic; (B) crouching; (C) filthy; (D) fretful; (E) flattened
543. B	**544. ANOMALOUS** (A) regular; (B) usual; (C) abnormal; (D) social
653. D	**654. CAPTIOUS** (A) protuberant; (B) ostentatious; (C) domineering; (D) faultfinding
763. A	**764. DURANCE** (A) penance; (B) imprisonment; (C) strength; (D) toughness
873. B	**874. GROMMET** (A) weight for sounding; (B) metal eyelet; (C) mischievous elf; (D) crystalline gem
983. C	**984. LUMBAR pertains to** (A) weight; (B) a crosspiece; (C) a joint; (D) the loins
1093. A	**1094. PERTINACIOUS** (A) persistent; (B) relevant; (C) saucy; (D) cohesive

1203. **A**	**1204. SIMPER** (A) sniff; (B) frown; (C) sob; (D) smirk
1312. **A**	**1313. ALEMBIC** (A) apparatus for distillation; (B) term in prosody; (C) plastic material; (D) synthetic jewel
1421. **D**	**1422. ELAN** (A) spirit; (B) name; (C) fruit; (D) vale
1530. **A**	**1531. MANNA** (A) spiritual food; (B) divine command; (C) idle chatter; (D) stale bread; (E) morning nap
1639. **A**	**1640. SAURIAN** (A) ape-like; (B) wicked; (C) winged; (D) lizard-like
1748. **C**	**1749. VALLEY is to GORGE as MOUNTAIN is to** (A) hill; (B) cliff; (C) pinnacle; (D) high; (E) altitude
1857. **D**	**1858. PHILIPPIC is to DEMOSTHENES as** **EUREKA is to** (A) Aristotle; (B) Phidias; (C) Archimedes; (D) Aristophanes
1966. **C**	**1967. BAY : PENINSULA : :** (A) safety : danger; (B) river : lake; (C) mountain : hill; (D) stand : sit; (E) sea : land
2075. **B**	**2076. SUBLIME** (A) below par; (B) highly praised; (C) extreme; (D) ignoble; (E) settled
2184. **B**	**2185. ————— that my uncle is, he can do just** **about everything.** (A) dipsomaniac; (B) factotum; (C) numismatist; (D) pachyderm

104. A	**105. COMMEND** (A) begin; (B) praise; (C) remark; (D) graduate; (E) plead
214. C	**215. FLUCTUATE** (A) fall; (B) impede; (C) waver; (D) rise; (E) hasten
324. D	**325. ONSLAUGHT** (A) waste; (B) ambition; (C) crime; (D) attack; (E) forgiveness
434. C	**435. STAGNANT** (A) inactive; (B) alert; (C) selfish; (D) difficult; (E) scornful
544. C	**545. ANOMALY** (A) nickname; (B) irregularity; (C) consistency; (D) homonym
654. D	**655. CARAFE** (A) glass water bottle; (B) means of transportation; (C) wineskin; (D) bony case covering back of animal
764. B	**765. EBULLIENT** (A) intoxicated; (B) heavy; (C) effervescent; (D) blustering
874. B	**875. GROUNDLINGS** (A) foundations; (B) underlings; (C) windfalls; (D) irregular soldiers; (E) forerunners
984. D	**985. MADRIGAL** (A) song; (B) wine; (C) maiden; (D) garland
1094. A	**1095. PERVASIVE** (A) inducing; (B) timely; (C) widespread; (D) indifferent

| 1204. D | 1205. **SIMULATE** |
| | (A) undermine; (B) feign; (C) bend to one's will; (D) improve upon |

| 1313. A | 1314. **ALIFORM** |
| | (A) wing-like; (B) symmetrical; (C) foliated; (D) many-sided |

| 1422. A | 1423. **EMPYREAL** |
| | (A) regal; (B) experimental; (C) pragmatic; (D) celestial; (E) poisonous |

| 1531. A | 1532. **MARQUETRY** |
| | (A) bas relief; (B) inlay; (C) carving; (D) design |

| 1640. D | 1641. **SAWBUCK** |
| | (A) antler; (B) bucksaw; (C) male deer; (D) rack |

| 1749. B | 1750. **MITOSIS is to DIVISION as OSMOSIS is to** |
| | (A) diffusion; (B) concentration; (C) digestion; (D) metamorphosis |

| 1858. C | 1859. **PROLOGUE is to EPILOGUE as PROTASIS is to** |
| | (A) epitome; (B) epigenesis; (C) apodosis; (D) apogee |

| 1967. E | 1968. **UGLY : APOLLO : :** |
| | (A) powerful : Zeus; (B) soft-spoken : Stentor; (C) strong : Hercules; (D) wily : Odysseus |

| 2076. D | 2077. **TERMAGANT** |
| | (A) fever; (B) quiet woman; (C) sea bird; (D) sedative; (E) squirrel |

| 2185. B | 2186. **His ———— features reminded me of the missing link.** |
| | (A) simian; (B) euphemistic; (C) vicarious; (D) vertiginous |

105. B	**106. COMPASSION** (A) rage; (B) strength of character; (C) forcefulness; (D) sympathy; (E) uniformity
215. C	**216. FOIBLE** (A) failing; (B) legend; (C) swoon; (D) reality
325. D	**326. OPIATE** (A) supposititious; (B) narcotic; (C) perform; (D) dictate
435. A	**436. STALEMATE** (A) deadlock; (B) excuse; (C) panic; (D) boredom; (E) contract
545. B	**546. ANTIPATHY** (A) aversion; (B) irritant; (C) phobia; (D) specific remedy
655. A	**656. CAREEN** (A) hurtle; (B) whirl around; (C) heel over; (D) move at breakneck speed
765. C	**766. ÉCLAT** (A) dance step; (B) brilliancy of achievement; (C) ardor; (D) high note
875. B	**876. HACKNEYED** (A) significant; (B) smart; (C) trite; (D) dishonest
985. A	**986. MALADROIT** (A) virulent; (B) rancorous; (C) unhandy; (D) sinister
1095. C	**1096. PETULANT** (A) childish; (B) spoiled; (C) fretful; (D) ill

1205. B	1206. **SINE QUA NON** (A) benefice; (B) impartiality; (C) necessity; (D) dissimulation
1314. A	1315. **ALIMENT** (A) digestion; (B) nutriment; (C) discharge; (D) waste
1423. D	1424. **ENATE** (A) fatigued; (B) related maternally; (C) out of order; (D) edible
1532. B	1533. **MAWKISH** (A) fumbling; (B) sickening; (C) awkward; (D) surly
1641. D	1642. **SCATOLOGICAL** (A) witching; (B) strewn; (C) obscene; (D) feline
1750. A	1751. **FINIAL is to PINNACLE as PEDIMENT is to** (A) basement; (B) footing; (C) gable; (D) obstruction; (E) pineal
1859. C	1860. **SAUTÉING is to COOKERY as FAGOTING is to** (A) juggling; (B) forestry; (C) embroidery; (D) medicine
1968. B	1969. **REWARD : PUNISHMENT :: ** (A) money : laughs; (B) medal : bravery; (C) bravery : cowardice; (D) North : South; (E) have : give
2077. B	2078. **SEDULOUS** (A) deceptive; (B) careless; (C) grassy; (D) hateful; (E) sweet
2186. A *Page* 212	2187. **For insisting on "It is I" instead of "It is me," he was charged with ————.** (A) calligraphy; (B) anomaly; (C) bellicosity; (D) preciosity

106. D	**107. COMPLACENCY** (A) anxiety; (B) satisfaction; (C) remorse; (D) dejection
216. A	**217. FOIL** (A) defeat; (B) punish; (C) accuse; (D) pray; (E) return
326. B	**327. OPPORTUNE** (A) self-confident; (B) rare; (C) frequent; (D) timely; (E) contrasting
436. A	**437. STATIC** (A) not moving; (B) referring to the state; (C) itemized; (D) clear; (E) pointed
546. A	**547. ANTIPHONAL** (A) opposite in meaning; (B) opposed; (C) tone-deaf; (D) responsive
656. C	**657. CARTE BLANCHE** (A) demerit; (B) symbol of cowardice; (C) unconditional authority; (D) press card
766. B	**767. ECLECTIC** (A) selecting; (B) secular; (C) clerical; (D) provincial
876. C	**877. HAGGLE** (A) wrangle; (B) bewitch; (C) erode; (D) juggle
986. C	**987. MALINGER** (A) prolong; (B) exasperate; (C) delay unnecessarily; (D) feign illness
1096. C	**1097. PHYSIOGNOMY** (A) physical geography; (B) configuration of the face; (C) art of healing diseases; (D) structure of the body

1206. C	**1207. SINUOUS** (A) delicate; (B) strong; (C) winding; (D) diseased
1315. B	**1316. ALTHEA** (A) mocking-bird; (B) flowering shrub; (C) balm; (D) luscious fruit
1424. B	**1425. ENFILADE** (A) a flaring up; (B) raking fire; (C) cataclysm; (D) canard
1533. B	**1534. MEGACEPHALY** (A) excessive largeness of head; (B) magnification of vision; (C) malformation of feet; (D) inordinate loss of hair
1642. C	**1643. SCHOLIAST** (A) commentator; (B) pretender to learning; (C) pedantic teacher; (D) founder of a philosophical school
1751. C	**1752. FLAMMABLE is to FIREPROOF as HALCYON is to** (A) calm; (B) heavenly; (C) stormy; (D) ancient; (E) handy
1860. C	**1861. NUMISMATIST is to COINS as CAMPANOLOGIST is to** (A) tours; (B) bells; (C) scouts; (D) politicos
1969. C	**1970. VIBRATE : UNDULATE : :** (A) sound : light; (B) shudder : quiver; (C) ripple : wave; (D) flutter : waver; (E) rattle : brandish
2078. B	**2079. ALFRESCO** (A) indoors; (B) art exhibit; (C) sidewalk cafe; (D) charcoal sketch
2187. D *Page* 214	**2188. In certain tropical areas, malaria is an —————— disease.** (A) endocrine; (B) introversive; (C) endemic; (D) interstitial

107. **B**	**108. COMPREHEND** (A) agree; (B) settle; (C) decide; (D) reprieve; (E) understand
217. **A**	**218. FORESTALL** (A) dispossess; (B) overshadow; (C) anticipate; (D) establish; (E) prepare
327. **D**	**328. OPPRESS** (A) conclude; (B) crush; (C) branch out; (D) alter; (E) stay within
437. **A**	**438. STIFLE** (A) smother; (B) yawn; (C) heighten; (D) promise; (E) strike
547. **D**	**548. APATHY** (A) sympathy; (B) anxiety; (C) assurance; (D) lethargy
657. **C**	**658. CATALYST** (A) recorder; (B) deputy; (C) deterrent; (D) accelerator
767. **A**	**768. ECOLOGY** (A) environmental study of organisms; (B) study of business; (C) doctrine of final causes; (D) science of family life
877. **A**	**878. HALCYON** (A) brilliant; (B) tranquil; (C) remembered; (D) ecstatic
987. **D**	**988. MANUMIT** (A) free from bonds; (B) cite for contempt; (C) write indelibly; (D) explicate
1097. **B**	**1098. PICARESQUE** (A) type of prose fiction; (B) Mexican sport; (C) Spanish dance; (D) school of painting

1207. **C**	**1208. SHAMBLES** (A) place of slaughter; (B) slum area; (C) thicket; (D) lameness in horses
1316. **B**	**1317. AMAIN** (A) windward; (B) steadfast; (C) forcibly; (D) starboard
1425. **B**	**1426. EPERGNE** (A) antique; (B) centerpiece; (C) highboy; (D) armoire
1534. **A**	**1535. MEPHITIC** (A) intoxicating; (B) noxious; (C) soporific; (D) tubercular
1643. **A**	**1644. SCIOLIST** (A) schoolman; (B) theologian; (C) interpreter; (D) pretender to scholarship; (E) organizer of knowledge
1752. **C**	**1753. GASOLINE is to PETROLEUM as SUGAR** **is to** (A) oil; (B) cane; (C) plant; (D) molasses; (E) sweet
1861. **B**	**1862. BRASS is to COPPER as PEWTER is to** (A) lead; (B) zinc; (C) silver; (D) bronze
1970. **C**	**1971. TRANSPARENT : TRANSLUCENT : :** (A) water : milk; (B) glass : water; (C) translucent : opaque; (D) clear : murky; (E) angry : choleric
2079. **A**	**2080. ALIMENT** (A) illness; (B) non-support; (C) sidewise motion; (D) wing-formation
2188. **C**	**2189. The day will come when ————— will look back on our time with a sense of superiority.** (A) teachers; (B) posterity; (C) scientists; (D) ancestors; (E) sophisticates

108. E	**109. COMPULSION** (A) contrition; (B) sympathy; (C) coercion; (D) kindness
218. C	**219. FORTHRIGHT** (A) direct; (B) constitutional; (C) unpleasant; (D) polite; (E) accidental
328. B	**329. ORNATE** (A) proper; (B) insincere; (C) stubborn; (D) birdlike; (E) adorned
438. A	**439. STOLID** (A) dishonest; (B) idiotic; (C) dirty; (D) dull; (E) tactless
548. D	**549. APHID** (A) plant juice; (B) thick honey; (C) small insect; (D) wild flower
658. D	**659. CATAMARAN** (A) raised structure on which a body is carried in state; (B) craft with twin parallel hulls; (C) monument to a person; (D) food fish
768. A	**769. ECUMENICAL** (A) metaphysical; (B) universal; (C) heretical; (D) non-clerical
878. B	**879. HANDWRITING ON THE WALL** (A) promise of greatness; (B) defiance of authority; (C) affirmation of faith; (D) pronouncement of doom
988. A	**989. MARE'S-NEST** (A) imaginary discovery that brings ridicule on the claimant; (B) eyrie; (C) well-padded stall; (D) horse van
1098. A	**1099. PINION** (A) lofty perch; (B) bird's wing; (C) supporter; (D) dance movement

1208. **A**	1209. **SHIBBOLETH** TURN TO PAGE 2 (A) watchword; (B) lisp; (C) weapon; (D) curse
1317. **C**	1318. **AMARANTHINE** TURN TO PAGE 2 (A) unfading; (B) serpentine; (C) pastoral; (D) greenish
1426. **B**	1427. **EPICENE** TURN TO PAGE 2 (A) feminine; (B) masculine; (C) belonging to both sexes; (D) unrelated to sex
1535. **B**	1536. **METATHETIC** TURN TO PAGE 2 (A) transposed; (B) emetic; (C) elastic; (D) unsympathetic
1644. **D**	1645. **SCUTAGE** TURN TO PAGE 2 (A) form of tax; (B) armor plate; (C) disposal plant; (D) decapitation
1753. **B**	1754. **MONARCHY is to KING as DEMOCRACY is to** (A) vote; (B) freedom; (C) people; (D) republic; (E) congress
1862. **A**	1863. **CAPE is to PROMONTORY as WADI is to** (A) river; (B) waterfall; (C) meadow; (D) fen
1971. **D**	1972. **ILLEGAL : CRIMINAL : :** (A) wish : deed; (B) civil : criminal; (C) misdemeanor : felony; (D) trespass : burglary; (E) crime : punishment
2080. **B**	2081. **ANIMADVERSION** (A) favorable remark; (B) soul sickness; (C) whole-heartedness; (D) opposing clique

109. C	110. COMPUTE TURN TO PAGE 1 (A) blame; (B) oppose; (C) limit; (D) reckon; (E) behave
219. A	220. FRAUDULENT TURN TO PAGE 1 (A) deceptive; (B) erosive; (C) horrifying; (D) demanding; (E) joking
329. E	330. OSTENSIBLE TURN TO PAGE 1 (A) vibrating; (B) odd; (C) apparent; (D) standard; (E) ornate
439. D	440. STRIFE TURN TO PAGE 1 (A) conflict; (B) weariness; (C) joy; (D) union; (E) strength
549. C	550. APHORISM TURN TO PAGE 1 (A) withering away; (B) blight; (C) metaphor; (D) proverb
659. B	660. CAUSERIE (A) legal deposition; (B) raceway; (C) chat; (D) warmth
769. B	770. EFFETE (A) patriarchal; (B) admirable; (C) worn out; (D) capable
879. D	880. HAUTBOY (A) chest of drawers; (B) musical instrument; (C) hat; (D) porter
989. A	990. MATUTINAL (A) growing and developing steadily; (B) pertaining to the morning; (C) pertaining to the afternoon; (D) established in a university as an annual event
1099. B	1100. PLACATE TURN TO PAGE 2 TOP FRAME (A) weaken; (B) conciliate; (C) filch; (D) scrape

Supplementary Aids
to Word Power

The Importance Of
A Good Vocabulary

Knowing the meanings of words is important to you for your future success—socially, scholastically, and in business.

It is obvious that you must have a reasonably wide choice of words at your command in order to get along well in your social environment. Moreover, statistics show that an adequate vocabulary ties up closely with scholastic and business success in our country. This was the valid conclusion of a scientific organization that tested the word knowledge of various groups. To measure vocabulary background, a test consisting of 150 words was administered. High school freshmen averaged 76 errors; college freshmen, 42 errors; college graduates, 27 errors; college professors, 8 errors; and "major executives," 7 errors. These "major executives" were individuals who held the post of president or vice-president in a well-rated business organization—and, mind you, they scored even higher than the college professors.

One of the executives tested had left school at the age of 14, and had had no formal education since. At first, he refused to take the test, for he felt that he would do poorly on it because of lack of schooling. When he was finally persuaded to participate in the experiment, he made only two errors. Several other groups were word-tested. The results strikingly revealed that there was a very close relationship between a large vocabulary and a high salary, a poor vocabulary and a low salary.

7 Simple Steps
To Increase Your Vocabulary

1. LEARN LATIN . . . don't get scared. We are referring to Latin roots, prefixes, and suffixes. Remember that approximately 70 per cent of our English words are derived from Latin and Greek.
2. TAKE WORD TESTS . . . such as those we have in the "frames" of this book.
3. STUDY WORD LISTS . . . These appear in some Review books.
4. READ . . . not only novels. Non-fiction is good, too . . . and don't forget to read newspapers.
5. LISTEN . . . to people who speak well. Tune in to worthwhile TV programs, also.
6. PLAY WORD GAMES . . . like Anagrams, Scrabble and Crossword Puzzles.
7. USE THE DICTIONARY . . . frequently and extensively.

This book will give you ample study and practice material in the first three steps listed:

LEARNING LATIN (AND GREEK)—On the next few pages you will find a listing of Latin and Greek stems, prefixes, and suffixes. Learn them. By so doing, you will build up your vocabulary effectively and speedily.

TAKING WORD TESTS—The "frame" section of the book has many word tests of different types.

USING WORD LISTS—We have some "beauties" beginning on page 230.

. . . .

Suggestion: Learn ten new words every day. Before a year elapses, you will have added to your present vocabulary over 3,000 usable words. What a tremendous difference this will make in your personality!

. . . .

Latin and Greek
Stems, Prefixes, and Suffixes

LATIN STEM	MEANING	EXAMPLE
ag, ac	do	agenda, action
agr	farm	agriculture
aqua	water	aqueous
bis	twice	binocular
cad, cas	fall	cadence, casual
cant	sing	chant
cap, cep	take	captive, accept
capit	head	capital
ced, cess	go, yield	precede, cession
celer	speed	celerity
cide, cis	kill, cut	suicide, incision
clud, clus	close	include, inclusion
cur, curs	run	incur, incursion
dec	ten	decimal
dent	tooth	indent
dict	say	diction
duc, duct	lead	induce, ductile
fact, fect	make	factory, perfect
fer, lat	carry	refer, dilate
fring, fract	break	infringe, fracture
frater	brother	fraternal
fund, fus	pour	refund, confuse
gen	produce	generate
greg	group	gregarious
gress, grad	move forward	progress, degrade
homo	man	homicide
ject	throw	reject
jud, jur	right	judicial, jury
junct	join	conjunction
lect, leg	read, choose	collect, legend
loq, loc	speak	loquacious, interlocutory
manu	hand	manuscript
mand	order	remand
mar	sea	maritime
mater	mother	maternal
med	middle	intermediary
min	lessen	diminution

LATIN STEM	MEANING	EXAMPLE
mis, mit	send	remit, dismiss
mort	death	mortician
mote, mov	move	remote, remove
naut	sailor	astronaut
nom	name	nomenclature
pater	father	paternity
ped, pod	foot	pedal, podiatrist
pend	hang	depend
plic	fold	implicate
port	carry	portable
pos, pon	put	depose, component
prehend	seize	reprehend
primus	first	primitive
reg, rect	rule, right	regicide, direct
rupt	break	eruption
scrib, scrip	write	inscribe, conscription
sec	cut	dissect
sed	remain	sedentary
sens, sent	feel	sensuous, presentiment
sequ	follow	sequential
spect	look	inspect
spir	breathe	conspire
stat, sist	stand	status, insist
tact, tang	touch	tactile, tangible
ten	hold	retentive
term	end	terminal
tract	draw	retract
vent	come	prevent
vert, vers	turn	divert, subversion
vict	conquer	evict
vid, vis	see	video, revise
voc	call	convocation
volv	roll	devolve

GREEK STEM	MEANING	EXAMPLE
anthrop	man	anthropology
arch	chief, rule	archbishop
astron	star	astronomy
auto	self	automatic
biblio	book	bibliophile
bio	life	biology
chrome	color	chromosome
chron	time	chronology
cosmo	world	cosmic
crat	rule	autocrat
eu	well, happy	eugenics
gamos	marriage	monogamous
ge	earth	geology
gen	origin, people	progenitor
graph	write	graphic
gyn	woman	gynecologist
homo	same	homogeneous
hydr	water	dehydrate
iso	equal	isothermal
logy	study of	psychology
macro	large	macrocosm
meter	measure	thermometer
micro	small	microscope
mono	one	monotony
onomy	science	astronomy
onym	name	synonym
pathos	feeling	pathology
philo	love	philosophy
phobia	fear	hydrophobia
phone	sound	telephone
pseudo	false	pseudonym
psych	mind	psychic
scope	see	telescope
soph	wisdom	sophomore
tele	far off	telepathic
theo	god	theology
thermo	heat	thermostat

PREFIX*	MEANING	EXAMPLE
ab, a	away from	absent, amoral
ad, ac, ag, at	to	advent, accrue, aggressive, attract
an	without	anarchy
ante	before	antedate
anti	against	antipathy
bene	well	beneficent
bi	two	bicameral
circum	around	circumspect
com, con, col	together	commit, confound, collate
contra	against	contraband
de	from, down	descend
dis, di	apart	distract, divert
ex, e	out	exit, emit
extra	beyond	extracurricular
in, im, il, ir, un	not	inept, impossible, illicit, irreparable, unreal
inter	between	interpose
intra, intro, in	within	intramural, introspective, intrude
mal	bad	malcontent
mis	wrong	misnomer
non	not	nonentity
ob	against	obstacle
per	through	permeate
peri	around	periscope
poly	many	polytheism
post	after	post-mortem
pre	before	premonition
pro	forward	propose
re	again	review
se	apart	seduce
semi	half	semicircle
sub	under	subvert
super	above	superimpose
sui	self	suicide
trans	across	transpose
vice	instead of	vice-president

* Latin and Greek.

SUFFIXES

SUFFIX*	MEANING	EXAMPLE
able, ible	capable of being	capable, reversible
al	relating to	fanatical
age	state of	storage
ance	relating to	reliance
ant, ent	one who	tenant, correspondent
ary	relating to	dictionary
ate	act	confiscate
ation	action	radiation
cle, ule, ling	diminutive	icicle, globule, duckling
cy	quality	democracy
ence	relating to	confidence
er, or	one who	adviser, actor
ic	pertaining to	democratic
ify	to make	solidify
ious	full of	rebellious
ist	one who	violinist
ize	to make like	harmonize
ment	result	filament
ness	state	goodness
ory	place where	dormitory
ous, ose	full of	melodious, verbose
tude	condition	rectitude
ty	condition	sanity

* Latin and Greek.

Words Often Heard But Not Often Understood

There are certain words that you often hear used by others in rather common, everyday conversation—yet you may not be quite sure of the exact meaning of these words. For example, you might have heard or seen the word *osteopath*. What does it mean? Or, you might actually have visited a *podiatrist*—or was he called a *chiropodist?*—in order to have a painful corn or bunion treated. What does the word mean? Then again, could you protect your own best interests by telling the difference between an *oculist,* an *optometrist,* and an *optician?* What do these words mean?

These questions and many others are answered in the word groups that follow.

DOCTORS AND RELATED PROFESSIONS

CHIROPODIST	Treats minor foot ailments
DERMATOLOGIST	Diagnoses skin ailments
GYNECOLOGIST	Specializes in the diseases that afflict women only
INTERNIST	Concentrates on the diseases of the internal organs
OBSTETRICIAN	Delivers babies
OCULIST (or OPHTHALMOLOGIST)	Treats the diseases of the eye
OPTOMETRIST*	Examines eyes, checks vision, measures eyes for glasses
ORTHODONTIST	A doctor of dentistry who specializes in the straightening of teeth
OSTEOPATH**	Attempts to cure diseases by methods including manipulative therapy

Note: *The *optometrist* is not an M.D. The *optician* is likewise not an M.D., but a technician who specializes only in the making of eye glasses.

** The *osteopath* (sometimes mistakenly considered a *chiropractor*) is a physician who is licensed to practice medicine and surgery in most states.

OTOLARYNGOLOGIST	Specializes in diseases of the ear and throat
PATHOLOGIST	Specializes in the nature and causes of disease
PEDIATRICIAN	Treats infants and young children exclusively
PHYSIOTHERAPIST***	Administers special treatment including heat, electricity, light, massage, and exercise
PODIATRIST	Another name for *chiropodist*
PSYCHIATRIST	Is literally a "mind doctor," diagnoses mental diseases

*** Or *physical therapist*. The *physiotherapist* need not be an M.D. The same is true of the *anesthetist,* who is, nevertheless, a highly trained assistant at major operations.

THEORIES ABOUT LIFE, ART, AND PHILOSOPHY

AGNOSTICISM	There are no definite answers to the meaning of God, life, nature, etc.
ALTRUISM	Man exists to help others
ATHEISM	There is no God
CHAUVINISM	No other country can compare with my own *in anything*
CONSERVATISM	Whatever is, is best. Let's not encourage changes
EGOISM	Man exists to help himself and nobody else
EPICUREANISM	The purpose of life is to avoid pain and to secure the maximum of pleasure
FATALISM	Everything in life happens according to blind fate, chance, luck, etc.
HEDONISM	Another word for *epicureanism*
IMPRESSIONISM	In art, the first impression, without elaborate detail, is the aim
JINGOISM	Force, war, aggression will solve all problems; might is right

231

LIBERALISM	Experiment and change will produce the best type of government
NATURALISM	In art, a representation of things as they really are, without frills
RADICALISM	Not just change, but *violent* change, will produce the best type of state
REALISM	Art or literature must conform to nature or to real life
ROMANTICISM	Art or literature must try to produce an idealistic or sentimental picture of nature or reality
SKEPTICISM	Since all knowledge is uncertain, let us suspend judgment about everything
STOICISM	Virtue and goodness lie in suffering mental and physical pain without complaint
SURREALISM	The subconscious mental activities (dreams, for example) may be represented by images presented without order or sequence
TOTALITARIANISM	The state is everything; the citizen is nothing. Man exists for the state alone

Note: There is no end to theories or to *isms*. Others you may wish to look into include: *pragmatism, empiricism, Dadaism, socialism, communism, imperialism, nihilism, colonialism, gradualism,* etc.

PERSONALITY IN A WORD

AMBIVERT	Satisfied both with oneself or with others
BLASE	Bored with people and with things
DIFFIDENT	Shy and timid
DOGMATIC	Positive or dictatorial in manner or speech
EBULLIENT	Overflowing with enthusiasm

EGOCENTRIC	Self-centered
EXHIBITIONIST	Desiring to act in front of others
EXTROVERT	Interested in things and people outside oneself
FASTIDIOUS	Difficult to please; fussy
GREGARIOUS	Wishing to be in the company of others at all times
INHIBITED	Unable to express oneself socially or publicly
INTROVERT	Interested or concerned with oneself only; unsociable
MASOCHISTIC	Finding pleasure in being abused or dominated
MISANTHROPIC	Hating or disliking mankind
QUIXOTIC	Idealistic and impractical
SADISTIC	Finding pleasure in abusing or dominating others
SANGUINE	Disposed to be hopeful; optimistic
SATURNINE	Gloomy
SUPERCILIOUS	Proud, haughty, contemptuous, snobbish
TRUCULENT	Savage or rough in character

SOME COMMON — AND UNCOMMON — PHOBIAS

ACROPHOBIA	Fear of high places
AGORAPHOBIA	Fear of wide-open spaces
AILUROPHOBIA	Fear of cats
ANGLOPHOBIA	Fear of all Englishmen and of everything English
AQUAPHOBIA	Fear of water
ASTRAPHOBIA	Fear of lightning
CERAUNOPHOBIA	Fear of thunder
CLAUSTROPHOBIA	Fear of close or closed places
CYNOPHOBIA	Fear of dogs
NYCTOPHOBIA	Fear of the dark
OCHLOPHOBIA	Fear of crowds
OPHIDIOPHOBIA	Fear of snakes
PHOTOPHOBIA	Fear of light
PYROPHOBIA	Fear of fire
XENOPHOBIA	Fear of the strange, the new, the different

SOME ABNORMAL MENTAL CONDITIONS*

ALEXIA	Loss of ability to read
AMNESIA	Loss of memory
APHASIA	Loss of the power of speech
CATATONIA	Alternate periods of stupor and activity
DEMENTIA	In psychology, any condition of deteriorating mentality
DEMENTIA PRAECOX	Insanity occurring in late adolescence
DIPSOMANIA	An uncontrollable desire for strong alcoholic drinks
ELECTRA-COMPLEX	A girl's unnatural attachment to her father
HYPOCHONDRIA	Fear, worry, or anxiety about one's health
INSOMNIA	Continuing inability to sleep
KLEPTOMANIA	An uncontrollable desire to steal
MANIC-DEPRESSION	Moods of violent excitement or elation followed by mental depression
MEGALOMANIA	An insane belief in one's own greatness
MELANCHOLIA	Continuing periods of gloom and depression
MONOMANIA	An obsession with but one idea
OEDIPUS-COMPLEX	A boy's unnatural attachment to his mother
PARANOIA	Mental unsoundness marked by persecution delusion
SCHIZOPHRENIA	Psychotic disorder marked by loss of contact with real world
SOMNAMBULISM	Walking or performing other actions in one's sleep
PYROMANIA	An insane desire to start fires

Note: Some of the conditions described herein may be temporary, and are therefore referred to as *neuroses;* the permanent or more serious ones are referred to as *psychoses.* In either case, it is not up to the layman to decide which condition belongs to the category of madness or insanity. As far as he is concerned, the terms are often used loosely, sometimes unsympathetically, and even humorously. The definitions given for the terms are *technically* correct.

SOME WORDS ABOUT THE AREAS OF KNOWLEDGE

ANTHROPOLOGY	The study of man's habits, history, culture
ARCHAEOLOGY	The study of ancient life
ASTROLOGY	The study of the influence of the stars upon human affairs
EGYPTOLOGY	The study of early Egyptian civilization
EMBRYOLOGY	The science dealing with the beginnings of life
ENTOMOLOGY	The study of insects
ETHNOLOGY	The study of the races of mankind
ETYMOLOGY	The study of the history and origin of words
GEOLOGY	The study of the structure and the forces of earth
GERONTOLOGY	The study of the aging processes in man
HOROLOGY	The study of time and the recording or measuring of time
MUSICOLOGY	The study of the history and theory of music
ORNITHOLOGY	The study of birds
PHILOLOGY	The study of the development of language
PSYCHOLOGY	The study of the mind and of human behavior
RADIOLOGY	The study of radioactive substances
SEISMOLOGY	The study of earthquakes
SELENOLOGY	The study of the moon
SOCIOLOGY	The study of the origin and development of human society
VOLCANOLOGY	The study of volcanoes

OTHER IMPORTANT BOOKS

DENTAL ADMISSION TEST

Complete guide for passing high a
entering the professional den
school of your choice. Thousands
practice questions and sample tes

paper: $6.

BAR EXAMS

Complete preparation for the all-
important examination for lawyers,
including actual recent bar exams
as well as hundreds of short-answer
and essay questions in adjective and
substantive law with answers to all
questions. There are also study sections for Problem Analysis Review as
well as a legal glossary.

paper: $5.00

NURSING SCHOOL ENTRANCE
   EXAMINATION

A "must" book for those seek
admission to all types of profe
sional nursing schools. It is design
to help applicants pass high on **t**
National League for Nursing P
Nursing and Guidance Examinatio
or on the **Psychological Corp.** E
trance Examination for Schools
Professional Nursing. Over 2,0
Nursing School Entrance Exam-ty
questions and answers on all phas
of the examination as well as samp
tests.

paper: $6.

SCORING HIGH ON READING TESTS

Thorough, easily understood material
in this book is designed to help can-
didates pass high on one of the most
difficult subjects that appears on
exams. Includes: question and answer
study sections on reading comprehension, interpretation, paragraphs,
sentence completion, literary mate-
rials, judgment and reasoning and a
concise course for faster, more effi-
cient reading and comprehension.

paper: $5.00

COLLEGE BOARD ACHIEVEMENT TEST
Preparation Books

The books in this series are designed to give college-bound high school students thorough preparation and practice material in the subjects required by hundreds of colleges as part of the College Entrance Examination. Each book contains: (1) complete sample tests closely following in format and level of difficulty the actual test given in the specific subject; (2) every type of question appearing on the actual test; (3) answers and, where appropriate, full explanations of the correct answers. The authors and consultants are all specialists in their fields.

The following titles have been published:

AMERICAN HISTORY & SOCIAL STUDIES	**GERMAN**
	LATIN
BIOLOGY	
	MATHEMATICS (LEVEL I)
CHEMISTRY	
	MATHEMATICS (LEVEL II)
ENGLISH COMPOSITION	
	PHYSICS
FRENCH	**SPANISH**

PRACTICE FOR SCHOLASTIC APTITUDE TESTS

Complete preparation for the Scholastic Aptitude Test, taken annually by over 800,000 students Practice in the Verbal and Math parts are included as well as "College Board" Vocabulary List, writing sample tips, and 2,000 SAT-type questions and answers. Sample SAT tests with answers given.

paper: $1.50

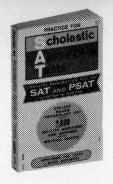

AMERICAN COLLEGE TESTING PROGRAM EXAMS

New book to assist the high school senior in entering the college of his choice where the American College Testing Program is the method of student selection. This book offers a sample examination for practice along with complete study sections in each phase of the exam.

Thousands of test-type questions are provided with complete answers for practice.

cloth: $8.00
paper: $5.00

SCORING HIGH ON PRELIMINARY SCHOLASTIC APTITUDE TESTS— NATIONAL MERIT SCHOLARSHIP TESTS

Book to help high school seniors pass the screening and qualifying exams and win a college scholarship.

paper: $4.00

BOOKS FOR EVERY INTEREST